D1043982

Responding to Evil

Responding to Evil

Joseph F. Kelly

LITURGICAL PRESS
Collegeville, Minnesota

www.litpress.org

Cover design by Greg Becker.

The Scripture quotations contained herein are from the New Revised Standard Version Bible, Catholic Anglicized Edition, © 1999, 1995, 1989, division of Christian Education of the National Council of the Churches of Christ in the United States of America, and are used by permission. All rights reserved.

© 2003 by the Order of Saint Benedict, Collegeville, Minnesota. All rights reserved. No part of this book may be reproduced in any form, by print, microfilm, microfiche, mechanical recording, photocopying, translation, or by any other means, known or yet unknown, for any purpose except brief quotations in reviews, without the previous written permission of the Liturgical Press, Collegeville, Minnesota 56321. Printed in the United States of America.

1	2	3	4	5	6	7	8

Library of Congress Cataloging-in-Publication Data

Kelly, Joseph F. (Joseph Francis), 1945–
    Responding to evil / Joseph F. Kelly.
      p. cm.
    Includes bibliographical references.
    ISBN 0-8146-2966-0 (alk. paper)
      1. Christian life—Catholic authors. 2. Good and evil. I. Title.

BX2350.3.K45 2003
231'.8—dc21   2003047607

To the McGinty family

With many thanks for many things

Contents

Acknowledgments

Peter Dwyer and Mark Twomey of the Liturgical Press invited me to write this book. My thanks to them for their confidence as well as their support.

There are several people at John Carroll University who aided this project: Doctors Matthew Berg and Richard Clark who introduced me to the new ideas on restorative justice; Dr. Paul Lauritzen, my department chairperson, who recommended me for a reduced load for writing; Dr. Nick Baumgartner, dean of the College of Arts and Sciences, and Dr. David LaGuardia, academic vice-president, who approved my reduced load; and Dr. Mary Beadle, dean of the Graduate School and Coordinator of Research, who authorized research grants to help me with this book. My sincerest thanks to all of them.

Dr. Kathleen O'Connor kindly allowed me to quote from an unpublished paper of hers, for which I am very grateful.

My special thanks go to my graduate assistant, Mrs. Dianne Alaimo, who read the manuscript and made many valuable suggestions for improving it, including several of the questions included at the end of the chapters. A portion of what may be good about this book belongs to her. The book's deficiencies are, of course, completely mine.

My most heartfelt gratitude goes to my wife Ellen, a loving and thoughtful spouse who made myriad sacrifices, large and small, so that I would have the time to write.

This book is dedicated to my old friend Thomas E. McGinty and his family, good friends, good people, and generous donors and supporters of educational and religious institutions. Their foundation, the McGinty Family Foundation, has done much to improve elementary and secondary education in the Greater Cleveland area, but it has especially helped impoverished children in inner city schools. "Truly, I say to you, that which you do unto the least of my brethren, that you do unto me" (Matt 25:40).

Joseph F. Kelly
University Heights, Ohio
January 20, 2003

Introduction

September 11, 2001

Like all Americans and many people of other countries, I was shocked and horrified by the terrorist attacks on our country on September 11, 2001. I had a nine o'clock class that morning. Some students came in saying that an airplane had crashed into the World Trade Center in New York City. All of us assumed that it had been an accident, and I recall mentioning that a plane had crashed into the Empire State Building in the 1930s. When class was over, I went into the hall where everyone was talking about the World Trade Center. I asked a colleague what had happened, and she replied, "Haven't you heard?" She told me briefly what was going on, and so I went to my office, got on to the Internet, and read about the attack.

Although I had no relatives or friends in the World Trade Center or in the Pentagon or on the flight that crashed in the Pennsylvania field, I did have a peripheral connection with the event. I have lived most of my life in Ohio, but I went to a boys' Catholic high school in New York City. I have not kept in-active-touch with the school but still receive the alumni newsletter. A few weeks after September 11 the newsletter arrived, reporting that twenty alumni, World Trade Center workers and New York City firefighters, had been killed in the attack. Graduation portraits of the victims were included. In actuality, I did not know any of them, but in a way, I knew all of them. They were just like me, middle-class boys who wanted to get an education, go on to a good college, and then lead fulfilling personal and professional lives. The graduation portraits were of sons and brothers; the people who died on September 11 were mostly husbands and fathers, leaving behind grieving, lonely widows and confused, frightened, vulnerable children, and all these alumni had done was to go to work in the morning.

In the days after the attack, all Americans followed the news carefully, trying to learn what had happened and, more importantly, trying

1

to *understand* what had happened. Pundits and commentators naturally had all the answers, even if they disagreed with one another, but their answers were rarely good enough. For most of us, this was not just a political or fanatically religious act. This act went beyond that, indeed, almost beyond comprehension for most of us. This was Evil, and on our doorstep.

Evil is not a popular topic, and most of us would rather not talk about it. We know it exists, and we know that people suffer from it, but unless it affects us directly, we like to keep it at a distance. But September 11 made it impossible to keep evil at a distance. *We* could have been in those buildings. *Our* families could be the grieving spouses, parents, and children. To be sure, time would pass, but those vivid images of the collapsing buildings, office workers jumping to their deaths, bodies being removed from the mountain of debris, will not be forgotten as long as we live. Evil had come to the front and center of our consciousness.

Evil presents a problem for all people, but especially for *theists*, that is, those of us who believe in God. And there are a lot of us. Surveys and polls repeatedly show that 93 to 95 percent of adult Americans believe in God. Since most of us come from Jewish, Christian, and, increasingly, Muslim backgrounds, we believe in the biblical God who is all-good and all-powerful, and that is why evil presents such a problem.

We believe that a good God does not want evil to occur. We believe that an omnipotent God can prevent evil from occurring. How then does evil happen? This is the basic framework of the intellectual question. But evil presents more than just an intellectual challenge. It presents a pastoral challenge with both personal and communal dimensions. What should we do about evil as individuals? What should we do about it as a group?

Let me tell you now that I make no claim to have all the answers. I truly wish I did. What follows rather is the product of years of reflection on the topic of evil, reflection honed by reading many books and articles on the topic but also by interaction with my university students and with people who have attended presentations and discussions at local churches in the Greater Cleveland area. They have all taught me a great deal about evil but also about the kinds of questions that people have regarding it. Many of their valuable queries and observations have found their way into this book and, while I will hardly claim that they have covered all the questions you might have, you can be sure that this book deals with more than just professors' inquiries. This book will treat evil not just as a theological or philosophical topic, but primarily as a lived problem that all of us have experienced.

We will address the topic from a Christian perspective, but it is not my intention to privilege a Christian understanding of evil. We all know the sufferings that God's Chosen People have endured from Pharaoh to the Holocaust and, like many Christians, I have learned much from Jewish approaches to evil. Furthermore, the fastest growing religion in the United States is Islam, yet in spite of our having Muslim friends, neighbors, and coworkers, too many of us still think of Islam as the religion of dangerous, anti-Western fanatics. Like Judaism, Islam has much to teach us about the problem of evil if we are only open to listen.

But I am a Christian and will thus approach the topic from the faith that I know and live. I am a Roman Catholic who will naturally draw heavily from the tradition of my Church, but I am also a dedicated ecumenist who appreciates other Christian traditions, and thus I hope that this little book will have value for all Christians.

1

What Evil Does to Us

Defining Evil

Few people in Christian history have had the faith of the apostle Paul. Called by a revelation from God, Paul defied the majority of his fellow Christians by insisting that he would bring the message of the new faith to the Gentiles. This meant that he had to travel constantly, often under difficult conditions and along dangerous roads. He met hostility, suspicion, skepticism, and derision. He survived a shipwreck, beatings, imprisonment, and constant misunderstanding. Pagan and Jewish mobs screamed for his blood, and he had to stand up for his views against two of the most influential figures in Early Christianity, Peter the apostle, leader of the Twelve, and James of Jerusalem, a relative of Jesus and head of the Jerusalem church (Gal 2:11). Nothing stopped Paul. When he said that faith could move mountains (1 Cor 13:2), he was not exaggerating.

But even an indestructible force like Paul could not fathom the mystery of Evil. In a reflective moment in his Epistle to the Romans (7:18-19), he lamented, "I can will what is right, but I cannot do it. For I do not do the good I want, but the evil I do not want is what I do." Here Paul sums up our dilemma. We know what is wrong, but we do it anyway. Why? What drives us to it?

What Paul devoted a small passage to, Augustine of Hippo (354–430), the great African saint and theologian, devoted his whole life. The problem of evil fascinated Augustine, who returned to it again and again in his writings, especially his books on Genesis. His most famous discussion of evil occurs in his spiritual autobiography *The Confessions*. He records that when he was a boy, he and a group of friends stole some pears from a nearby orchard. They did not eat the pears; they did not save them; they did not give them to animals. They just discarded them.

They derived no benefit from this theft. Yet they did it, and Augustine wants to know why.

Augustine wrote *The Confessions* when he was in his forties, literally decades after the event. If we are not careful, we could easily write off his interest in the theft as a sad example of over-scrupulosity. After all, he was a boy, and boys do lots of stupid things. Besides, he just stole a few pears; it is not as if he and his friends chopped down the orchard and ruined the owner financially. This is clearly a minor incident, but when one of the greatest minds in Christian history takes something this seriously, it is worth a second look.

When we take that second look, we understand why Augustine remained fascinated by his boyhood misdemeanor. As a citizen of Roman Africa at a time when the Empire was crumbling under the weight of corruption, widespread poverty, local tyranny, and barbarian invasions, Augustine knew that a couple of kids stealing some pears was hardly an earthshaking matter. But he was not interested in the substance of the act, which was minor, but in the very act itself. Why did he do it? Why did he steal just to steal? Why did he do something that did not benefit him materially? If someone steals a lot of money in order to be rich, that would make some (dishonest) sense, but to do something wrong just to do it, that was the problem.

It is strangely comforting to know that we are not alone in wondering about evil and that even the greatest names in the history of the Church have shared our dilemma, but that does not make the dilemma go away. In the next chapter we will see how Augustine and others tried to explain the problem of evil, but for now it would be good to define evil in order to get our bearings.

Evil joins many other terms in being ultimately indefinable. How could we define love, success, loyalty, civilization, or education, among many others, in such a way that no one would disagree with our definition? At my university (John Carroll), we not only debate what education is but also what Jesuit education is. (Frankly I am not sure what we would talk about at faculty convocations if we ever did figure that one out.) But if we cannot define such terms precisely, we can recognize them when we see them. Anyone looking at a young mother holding a newborn baby can see the love between the two, just as we can see the love between an elderly wife and husband who have shared decades of life together.

And, of course, we can recognize evil. We can certainly see it in events like September 11, and we can see it in lesser crimes as well. All we need do is pick up a newspaper. But evil goes far beyond crimes. Unfortunately, we can see it in so many petty ways in the behavior of others and, most disappointingly, in the behavior of ourselves. How many times have we found ourselves thinking, "I should never have said that. I should have realized how much it would hurt her feelings." Or, conversely, "Why did I just sit there? Why didn't I say something, to show him I'm supportive? He deserved better of me, and I let him down." And we can all multiply these examples. However indefinable evil might be, we can certainly recognize it.

But a book on evil must have at least a working definition of the term. For that we will turn to Jeffrey Burton Russell, a foremost authority on evil. In his book *The Devil* (p. 17), Dr. Burton writes, "the essence of evil is abuse of a sentient being, a being that can feel pain. It is the pain that matters. Evil is grasped by the mind immediately and immediately felt by the emotions; it is sensed as hurt deliberately inflicted." We will abbreviate this to "the deliberate imposition of suffering by a human being upon another sentient being."

"Deliberate" means that the person committing the evil deed knows what she or he is doing. Many people hurt others unintentionally, sometimes even more than they could have done intentionally, but such acts are not evil.

"Imposition of suffering" means that the action harms a sentient being. The harm need not be physical. A man who would never strike a woman could harm his spouse by infidelity; a woman who would never hit her children can abuse them with cutting remarks. And too many of us impose suffering upon ourselves without realizing what we are doing.

The phrase "sentient being" would have surprised previous generations who would have expected to see "another human being," but humans can inflict harm upon animals, not just as individuals but also as entire species as we drive more and more of them into extinction. Many modern people who practice ecospirituality and environmental ethics would add the living planet to the list as well. Although many people think of God as impervious to what we do, we should remember that those who love are vulnerable to hurt. God loves us, and we can offend and disappoint God when we go against his will or reject his love.

This definition deals with moral evil, the interaction of humans with other sentient beings. But people also speak of natural evil, the harm done to us by natural forces, such as hurricanes or tornadoes. These can be very harmful, but are they really "evil"? Today most people consider the harm done by natural forces to be just natural phenomena. God can act in our physical lives, but to call a storm "evil" confuses and cheapens the term. For this book, then, we will deal with moral evil.

Slide e
natural evil
ontic evil
moral evil

The Forms That Evil Takes

In the twenty-first century we are accustomed to barely being able to keep up with all the new knowledge that becomes available, especially via technology, and it is not just *what* to know but *how* to know it. I will never forget how my son referred to my three-year-old computer as a "dinosaur." There I was, still trying to figure out how to use some its multifarious programs, and he was telling me that it was already outdated. No doubt that scene was reenacted in countless other households. I mention it because it also illustrates another feature of our current learning situation, and that is that it helps to be young if you want to grasp this ever-changing technological era. The "Wisdom of the Ages" does not speak very loudly today.

But if the amount of knowledge and the ways of getting it have changed, some of the problems we humans face have not. Many of those problems can be solved by modern technological advances, for example more efficient production of crops and delivery of food could help solve food shortages in the Third World, but many of those problems persist because human beings have not advanced morally. Third World people often endure hunger because dictatorial governments use foreign food aid as a lever for power or because internal strife prevents food aid from reaching the hungry or because rich countries prefer to make friends with Third World governments by giving them weapons instead of feeding the hungry. The technology has advanced, but human nature has stayed the same. Our perennial problems are human ones.

Because they are human ones, we can learn how to deal with them by looking not just at our contemporaries but also at the "Wisdom of the Ages," the many people who thought seriously and deeply about the human condition. In the Sermon on the Mount (Matthew 5–7), Jesus enunciated the eight beatitudes, guides to living in harmony with others. The Buddha taught nonviolence and respect for life. The Jewish prophets insisted that caring for the poor counted for more than following formal religious guidelines. All generations have produced sensitive and perceptive thinkers who have meditated on the problem of evil as our generation is doing. We will do well to look at the "Wisdom of the Ages" on this perennial human problem and the powerful insights into the nature of evil that the they have given us as well as a modern writer's reimaging of a biblical book.

The Book of Genesis

In the opening chapters of the book of Genesis (1–11), one finds the ancient Hebrew etiological myth. An *etiology* is a story of how something began. Since the world obviously exists, virtually every society has an account of its creation. While the biblical Genesis account is best known to us in the West, other Western cultures have produced creation accounts. The Greeks spoke of the cosmos emerging from the primeval chaos and of the mating of Mother Earth (Gaia) and Father Sky (Uranus), while the ancient Scandinavians believed in the great world tree Yggdrasil that supported all creation on its branches. As we have gotten to know and respect many other cultures, we have learned of many other such stories, such as the Pueblo Indians of the American Southwest who tell of different races of people emerging from Mother Earth.

Creation myths are found among all ancient and primitive peoples, and we should not be surprised to find one in ancient Israel. But many Christians object to this idea. After all, does not the word "myth" mean some fantastic story about gods and goddesses and heroic humans? Surely, the ancient Israelites did not have such things. This is true if we limit the notion of myth to a very narrow compass, but what biblical scholars understand as myth is a story that humans create to give shape to forces they cannot understand. For ancient and primitive peoples, myths have great power precisely because they enable us to come in contact with the divine.

In a way, we could say that most of our ideas about God are myths. We believe that God is beyond all human categories of understanding, but, of course, we cannot pray to a being about whom we have no understanding. We believe that God is a person, but all persons we know have gender, age, ethnicity, and many other traits, and it is impossible for us to imagine a person without those attributes. Thus when we portray God as a person, we in the West have traditionally portrayed him as a middle-aged or elderly white man, usually with a beard, reflecting Western ethnicity but also cultural and patriarchal prejudices— if men are naturally superior to women, clearly the divine being *must* also be male.

Sometimes we get even more specific. The famous ninth-century Irish manuscript the Book of Kells portrayed Jesus with red hair and green eyes! The obvious intent was to make him more real to the Irish Christians, but we can see the point. We cannot understand the divine nature, but we need to have an image of God so we can pray to him, and we usually make that image so that God looks like one of us. Think of how often Western Christians are surprised when they see God with Asian or African features in the Christian art of those areas.

So there is nothing wrong with an ancient people, even God's Chosen People, having myths. In fact, it is what we would expect. Recognizing this, we also recognize that the opening chapters of Genesis do not give us a physical description of how the world began. This is the view of Christian fundamentalists, and I simply cannot deal adequately with their views in a small book. I would simply say that Jews, Catholics, Orthodox, and mainline Protestants are united in rejecting this view. They do not believe that Genesis 1–11 contains a physical account of the world's beginnings. They do, however, believe that it contains divinely revealed truths that can teach us a great deal if we approach them the right way. And that is what we will do with evil.

The sections of Genesis that deal with evil are chapters 3 and 4. Chapter 3 deals with the serpent's tempting of Adam and Eve to eat the forbidden fruit and of the consequences of that act; chapter 4 shows the further consequences of evil in the lives of Adam and Eve's two sons, Cain and Abel.

The story of Adam and Eve begins in chapter 2 when God has created a perfect natural world, the Garden of Eden which bloomed with plants and was surrounded by rivers. It is easy to see why an ancient people living in a largely dry, desert environment would picture the ideal world that way. God placed humans and animals in the garden, and he gave the humans the task of tilling the garden and taking care of it, not, as has frequently been believed, to dominate and do whatever they wanted with or to it. Eden represented what religious scholars call a *cosmos,* a place of harmony where the will of God is observed. But a cosmos is not a free gift. Those living in the cosmos have obligations. In pagan polytheistic societies this often meant offering animal sacrifices to the gods or observing the requirements of ritual purity, but in Genesis the obligation took the form of a simple command: Do not eat of the fruit of the Tree of the Knowledge of Good and Evil, a command that Adam and Eve had no trouble keeping until . . . .

In ancient Near Eastern Semitic mythology serpents represented *chaos,* the destructive force which worked against cosmos. Although we understand the serpent in the Garden of Eden as a snake, the serpent in pagan mythology was often a dragon or sea serpent. In fact, the sea serpent appears in the Bible itself. In Psalm 74 we read that God "broke the heads of the dragons on the waters" and "crushed the heads of Leviathan," a sea monster with many heads (vv. 13-14). The book of Job speaks of Behemoth (40:15), and Isaiah portrays God piercing the dragon Rahab (51:9). Later tradition would turn the Genesis serpent into the devil, but Genesis itself never uses that term, seeing the serpent rather as a symbol of chaos.

The notion of chaos probably has more value for us than the devil because the demonic implies a supernatural opponent, whereas Genesis makes it very clear that the problem lay with Adam and Eve who were not outwitted by a superior being but who gave in to evil longings.

The serpent promises Adam and Eve that if they eat the fruit of the tree, they will "be like God, knowing Good and Evil," possibly an ancient idiom meaning that they would know opposites, that is, know everything, so they will be like God by being omniscient. But the key phrase is "to be like God." Adam and Eve, if they obey God, can be perfect human beings, but they are not satisfied with that. They want to be more—in itself not necessarily a bad thing—but they want to be more than they had a *right* to be because no human has the right to play God. The ancient Greeks had a word for this, *hubris* or pride. This does not mean pride in the sense that all of us take pride in a job well done or we are proud of a relative or friend who wins an award. It means what Genesis means—people who want to be more than they have a right to be. The Greek prince Bellerophon rode the flying horse Pegasus to the summit of Mount Olympus, the home of the gods, who struck Bellerophon down to earth where he belonged. Another Greek prince named Phaethon drove the chariot of the sun, which only the sun god could do, and he, too, met with disaster.

So Genesis, the first book we encounter in the Bible, shows us what evil does to us. The serpent lies to Adam and Eve, but they in turn lie to themselves. Why? Because they want to. Not satisfied with God's gifts, they want to be like the giver. They do not look at the good that they have and thank God for it. They devalue what he has done for them, preferring *hubris* to goodness. They turn their backs on the good of God's personhood for a false value. How often have we denied the goodness of a person for the supposed goodness of a thing? A third-century Egyptian Christian writer named Origen believed that all sin begins with *hubris,* and he was right. When we sin, that is, when we knowingly do what is wrong, we, like Adam and Eve, act like God. We decide that our will takes precedence over God's will, that we will lie instead of tell the truth, that we will cheat instead of study.

This delusion takes other forms. Adam and Eve believe that they could hide what they have done. Sounds familiar, does it not? Rather like all the public figures who try to cover up what they have done, only to learn that the coverup becomes more difficult and complicated than the original offense. They soon find out that the simple act of "fessing up" and asking for forgiveness would have been so much simpler, more ethical, and more spiritually rewarding. But, as the anonymous Jewish author of Genesis shows us, when we have committed a wrong, we usually do not move on to the laudable stage of admitting what we have done so that we can set about making amends to those whom we have hurt.

When God, who is walking in the garden in the cool of the day—what a wonderful image!—looks for Adam and Eve, whom he loves and whose company he wants to share, they hide from him. When he calls them, Adam says they hid because they were naked—a natural reaction in a world of sin and shame but not in the Garden of Eden where our first parents walked in what the great English poet John Milton called "naked majesty," that is, in pure, simple goodness. God senses something is wrong and promptly asks Adam and Eve, "Have you eaten from the tree of which I commanded you not to eat?" Adam promptly tries to weasel out of what he has done by blaming *not just Eve but also God himself.* "The woman, whom *you* gave to be with me, she gave me fruit from the tree, and I ate." His partner learns quickly and shifts the blame to the serpent. "The serpent beguiled me, and I ate." All in all, a sad affair. They had evidence of God's love, but they did not trust it. Had they done so, they could have asked his forgiveness, but they chose evil once, then again, and then again.

Punishment soon followed; God expelled them from the Garden of Eden. Yet he continued to love them and blessed them with two sons, Cain and Abel. But the harm had been done; the evil genie could not go back into the bottle. Adam and Eve had disobeyed and lied; because of jealousy, their son Cain would murder his brother Abel. With horror humankind's first parents watched their sin infect others; with horror they realized that evil, once let loose, cannot be restrained. From disobedience to murder in a single generation! And it did not stop there. Genesis 4 gives an account of Cain's descendants, one of whom, Lamech, claimed that he would avenge himself seventy-sevenfold on anyone who injured him. From an almost immeasurably small beginning, the serpent's lie to Eve, evil had now come to dominate the world.

Some people think that Genesis loses its power unless we accept it as an historically or physically true account of the world's beginnings. I must disagree. A story need not be factual to have value. Let us remember that Jesus often taught in parables. Genesis 1–11 may be an etiological myth, but it is one of great power and sophistication. Its anonymous Jewish author has given us a solid picture of how evil works and how it affects us. As a teacher I have gone over Genesis with students many times, and it still rewards a careful reading, no matter how familiar one is with it.

The Gospel According to Luke

Many other books of the Hebrew Bible deal with evil, often brilliantly, but since I want to survey authors from different periods in history, it is time to move on to the New Testament, which, of course, presents us with a similar problem—so many of its books deal with evil. One thinks of the Gospel of John with its superb imagery of light and dark or of the Apocalypse with its cosmic battle between the forces of good and evil.

But my choice has fallen upon an old friend Luke, the subject of my doctoral dissertation years ago and still my favorite among the New Testament writers.

And not just mine. Many Christians like Luke because more than any of the other Gospel writers, Luke deals with joy and prayer and forgiveness. The joy appears right in the beginning with the Infancy Narrative when the angel Gabriel brings to both Mary and Elizabeth (via her husband Zachary) the joyful news that they will have children, sons who will grow up to be great men. But if this seems too narrow, since both Mary and Elizabeth are exceptional figures, let us recall that when the angel appeared to the shepherds, lowly people like us, he said, "Behold I bring you tidings of great joy." And only Luke has this account.

Praying also appears early on since Zachary, whose story opens the Gospel, is in the Temple offering sacrifice, a central form of prayer at that time, when the angel comes to announce the conception of John. Prayer appears at another "beginning," the beginning of Jesus' public career when he accepts baptism from John the Baptist. Luke (3:21) tells us "when Jesus had also been baptized and *was praying*. . . ." Significantly, all four evangelists recount the story of Jesus and John, but only Luke reports that Jesus was praying.

For those concerned with evil, what could be more important than forgiveness? Luke provides the classic example, the "Good Thief." All four Gospels recount that Jesus was crucified between two criminals. Mark and Matthew tell us that the criminals who died with Jesus taunted him about calling upon divine power to save himself. John mentions the two criminals but says nothing about them. Luke, and only Luke, tells us that, in his final moments, one of the criminals came to his senses. Unlike Adam and Eve, he admits his wrongdoing. ". . . we (meaning the other criminal and himself) indeed have been condemned justly, for we are getting what we deserve for our deeds . . ." (23:41). Recognizing the goodness of Jesus, he asks simply, "Jesus, remember me when you come into your kingdom." He receives the wonderful reply when the suffering and dying Jesus performs one last act of kindness, assuring this man, "Truly, I tell you, today you will be with me in Paradise." Who could hope for more?

I hope that you will agree with me that a gospel that emphasizes joy, prayer, and forgiveness, which we all need, will be a good place to see what evil does to us. Let us look at Luke's account of Satan's temptation of Jesus (4:1-13).

The temptation gets us into the difficult territory of Jesus' true humanity, a problem for many Christians but especially for those of us who believe that Jesus was also truly divine. The Gospels (Matthew, Mark, and Luke have an account of this) say simply that the devil "tempted" him or that he "was tempted" by the devil. Yet we also read in the Epistle to the Hebrews (4:15) that Jesus is like us in all things except sin. So if he never sinned, does that mean that he was therefore never tempted, and the devil simply banged his head against stone? That seems to be the logical conclusion, yet must it be? If it were, why did the evangelists not come out and say that "the devil tried to tempt him" or, even more strongly, "the devil foolishly believed that he could tempt him"? But instead, they say directly that he was tempted by the devil.

This apparent problem can be solved by recognizing an important fact about temptation, and that is that there is nothing wrong with it. We encounter temptations all the time, such as food that makes us want to cheat on a diet or an important game on television that makes us want to put off working. Temptations can be strong. The Irish writer Oscar Wilde wittily pointed out that "The only way to get rid of a temptation is give in to it." He is probably right, but the problem with temptation does lie precisely in giving in to it.

Since I am a teacher, let me use an academic example. Instead of studying for an important test, a student goes out the night before with some friends. Why not, he thinks. You are only in college once, and who wants to miss out on a good time? But morning always comes, and there is still the exam. Staring at the questions, the student quickly finds out that he should have studied. The test is difficult, and his grade is sinking fast. Then he notices that the smart student in the next row has not covered her paper very well, and he can read her answers. Suddenly he has discovered a perfect way to pass the test.

This all sounds pretty bad, but, if we look carefully, we realize that the student has not yet done anything wrong. He was lazy and he procrastinated, but nothing more. He is being tempted, sorely tempted, but until he gives into the temptation and starts to copy the other student's answers, he has not cheated. Will he? In the optimistic spirit of Luke's Gospel, let us assume our hypothetical student is deep down a good guy. He admits to himself that he put himself in this predicament, and he will not cheat to get himself out of it. In this minor battle between good and evil, good wins a round.

This little parable illustrates an important point. There is no sin in being tempted, so maybe we can accept the Gospel account and give credit to the human Jesus who faced up to and overcame temptations, very insidious temptations propagated, the Gospel tells us, by the Prince of Darkness himself.

The temptations occurred after Jesus had been on what we call today a personal retreat. "Jesus, full of the Holy Spirit, returned from the Jordan (that is, from his baptism by John) and was led by the Spirit in the wilderness, where for forty days he was tempted by the devil. He ate nothing at all during those days, and when they were over, he was famished."

His hunger formed the setting for the first temptation. "The devil said to him, 'If you are the Son of God, command this stone to become a loaf of bread.'" Note that the first temptation occurs on the physical level, and it involves immediate gratification. Here is something that we want but do not have, so we do what we have to do to get it, even if that means doing something wrong. But, Luke adds, Jesus was famished. He did not just want food, he needed it. Besides, who would get hurt by his turning a stone into bread? All that is true, but Luke's point is that the very per-sonification of evil wants him to do that minor miracle. On its own, turn-ing stone to bread would not be wrong, but to do so at Satan's bidding would be wrong. Jesus refuses, citing, like the devout Jew he was, the book of Deuteronomy (8:3), the Law given by his Father to his people.

Enticing as base, physical temptations might be, most of us can over-come them. After all, if we are going to sin, it might as well as be for something important, or at least that is how Satan reasons in the Gospel. Not in the least deterred by his initial failure, "the devil led him up and showed him in an instant all the kingdoms of the world. And the devil said to him, 'To you I will give their glory and all this authority; for it has been given over to me, and I give it to anyone I please. If you, then, will worship me, it will all be yours.'" That is quite a reward for a simple bending of the knee.

Before getting to Jesus' response, we should consider the devil's claim that all these kingdoms have been given over to him. Given by whom? First, possibly by nobody because the devil is the primeval liar, and maybe the reader should not take this claim seriously. Second, they were certainly not given by God, but rather these kingdoms passed into Satan's power through sin. We must recall that the earliest Christians believed the world to be in the power of evil; that is why Jesus had to re-deem it. But the point of the story is the nature of the temptation, made possible by Satan's control of this world, a control that Jesus would take away from him.

People enjoy having money, and most enjoy having power. Many people want these to do good, such as donating to a charity or righting a wrong, but no one can doubt that money and power have an intrinsic appeal apart from desires to do good. How easy life can be when we can afford things, and how pleasurable it can be to see that things we want to be done get done. Yet these attitudes can go to our heads. If money can be good, can we ever have enough of such a good? Maybe we should be less generous and hold onto more of our money. Since we are using our power only for the good, how can anyone disagree with what we are doing? What is the matter with those people who do not want to go along with what we want? Maybe we should start throwing our weight around a little more. Luke knew what he was doing when he placed wealth and power in the second temptation.

But again for Jesus, the price was too high. He had a mission to liberate the world, not dominate it. He had to do his Father's will, not Satan's. To give in to this temptation would betray his mission and his God. Again quoting Deuteronomy (6:13), he turns down the second temptation.

Now Luke shows his literary artistry via the third temptation. All of us have done what Jesus did, overcoming base physical temptations and even overcoming more appealing ones to wealth and power. A lot of other people could not have done what we did. We really are good, aren't we? And thus the third temptation, spiritual pride.

"Then the devil took him to Jerusalem, and placed him on the pinnacle of the Temple, saying to him, 'If you are the Son of God, throw yourself down from here, for it is written, "He will command his angels concerning you, to protect you," and, "On their hand they will bear you up, so that you will not dash your foot against a stone."'" Before we get to the temptation, let us note that the devil is now quoting Scripture. That seems a bit ludicrous, almost amusing, but for Luke this story has a deadly seriousness about it. Here the evangelist shows us how evil adapts to new situations. Just because we have overcome it once or twice, it does not admit defeat. Realizing that Jesus relies on Scripture for his values, Satan tries to justify his temptation with not one but two scriptural citations (both from Psalm 91), a good example of Satan's not just updating his approach but also using something good to induce evil.

Luke has recognized a fundamental *moral flaw in good people,* which most of us are. If we are not careful, we become like the Pharisee in the famous parable—also found only in Luke: "The Pharisee . . . was praying thus, 'God, I thank you that I am not like other people: thieves, rogues, adulterers, or even like this tax collector [publican]. I fast twice a week; I give a tenth of all my income [a tithe]'"(18:11-12). We must note that Luke never even implies that the Pharisee is lying. Just the reverse. He is telling the truth. He is indeed not like most other people, and he does carry out those religious practices he mentions. He is a basically good man, and many of us would be glad to know someone like that. His problem, though, is that he has allowed his rule-following standard of goodness to keep him from noticing his faults. His "prayer" consists of a series of congratulations to himself. He fails to see that *in front of God* none of us, not the best of us, not the greatest of saints, is faultless. We are all sinners, and we must never forget that. We all know that those who donate to charities are doing a better thing than those who hoard their funds to buy bigger and bigger houses or cars; if we did not believe that, we ourselves would not give. We can and should take a legitimate satisfaction at having performed a good act, but we cannot let it go to our heads. The moment we do, we have spoiled the value of the very good we have done.

Luke understood this, and he saved spiritual pride for the last temptation precisely because it could grow out of overcoming other temptations. Jesus recognized this, and he refused to give in. Throwing himself off the pinnacle of the Temple and being caught up by angels would have been an impressive miracle, but to what purpose? In the Gospels Jesus performed miracles after people had demonstrated their faith and for a good purpose. Mark tells us that when Jesus encountered disbelief in his home town, "he could do no miracle there" (6:5), not that he was unable to work physical marvels but that he did miracles *because* people had faith in him, not to amaze them into it. Luke tells us that when Pontius Pilate sent Jesus to Herod Antipas, the ruler of Galilee for the Romans, Herod "was hoping to see him perform some sign" (23:8). Although Jesus would use his power to cure illnesses, he did not "do tricks" for anyone.

That is the case of the third temptation. He would be demonstrating his power for no other reason than to demonstrate that he had such power—pure spiritual pride. Again citing Deuteronomy (6:16), Jesus refuses the final temptation.

The temptation scene is a Lukan gem, showing us how evil works on us. First, it appeals to our baser desires for instant gratification. Next, it moves to the level of wealth and power, forces which would make us important people in the world. But if we overcome these two, evil is waiting with its third and most insidious temptation, hitting us where we are weakest, in our satisfaction with the good we have done. In the words of a famous first-century Galilean rabbi, who was teaching his disciples how to pray, "lead us not into temptation but deliver us from evil."

Augustine of Hippo

St. Augustine of Hippo (356–430), a native of North Africa, played an immensely influential role in the development of Western notions of evil. Most directly, he propagated the traditional Christian concept of original sin, a phrase he used for the first time in history in 393. This does not sound very important. After all, Adam and Eve did sin when they disobeyed God and ate the forbidden fruit, and since this was the first time this had ever happened, this was the original sin. True, but the term means more than just chronological primacy. For Augustine, original sin forever corrupted the basic character of human nature.

He wrote constantly about original sin, so we can consider only some of his views. Like other ancient Christians, he accepted the physical and historical existence of Adam and Eve, of the Garden of Eden, and of the serpent. Augustine believed that original sin caused a break between nature and us. We lived in harmony with the natural world in the Garden of Eden, but that we destroyed that harmony by wanting to be like nature's creator. Even if we do not believe that by eating a piece of fruit two prehistoric people severed our relationship with the natural world, we can still appreciate Augustine's sense that our oneness with nature, symbolized by the Garden of Eden, no longer exists. Augustine saw the break in terms of our having to fear wild animals, but we can see it in the disrespect we have for the natural world. We are no longer part of it; rather we are masters of it. To be sure, when hurricanes or blizzards strike, nature temporarily reasserts its power, but, in the long run, we are asserting our power over it. More of the natural world disappears so that we can build bigger and bigger houses even as we have smaller and smaller families to live in them. We worry about how long fossil fuel will last as we drive vehicles that guzzle more and more gas. We enjoy seeing animals in their natural habitats as we progressively destroy those habitats.

That catalogue of woes is not meant to be as negative as it probably sounds. I belong to a local environmental organization, and my wife and I practice wildlife gardening, so we really believe that all is not lost. But the problem is a serious one for our environment, and Augustine, in his own way, realized it. Oddly enough, his view has a modern ring. In the nineteenth century, when Darwinian evolution changed our view of our relationship to nature, many people complained that evolution had brought us down low, down to the level of animals. We were the masters of the world, above the animals and plants because of our reason, and now evolution suggested that we too were subject to all the processes of nature. "Exactly! And all to the good," we would say in the twenty-first century.

Our reason does distinguish us from other creatures on the planet, but, in a very basic way, we are no different from those creatures. What Augustine sensed was that God had created *all* life on earth, and this divine foundation gave all life an underlying unity. The sin of pride caused us to think we are separate from the rest of life, and that attitude impacted the rest of life on earth. Our environmental problems do not have a social or economic base but rather a spiritual one. The biggest problem facing the natural world is Western materialism, our endless desire to have more and more, regardless of what it does to the world. Obviously Augustine could not have foreseen anything like that, but his many writings about the Garden of Eden do warn us about the consequences of divorcing ourselves from the natural world.

Another way in which Augustine showed us what evil does to us is his insistence that evil is a constant presence in our lives and shows up even in little matters. Before he wrote on the topic, Christian scholars who thought about evil wrote about things like demonic assaults or the conflict between paganism and Christianity. Augustine did all of this, too, but his theology of original sin, the notion that human nature is fundamentally corrupted by it, led him to see the extent to which evil perverts our lives. Earlier in this chapter we saw his fascination with what drove him to steal pears when he was a boy. We do not want to turn petty wrongs into major evils, but we must credit Augustine for alerting us to how evil is a constant presence in our lives and one for which we must always be on guard. His emphasis on our divorce from nature retained the notion of cosmic evil, but he also showed us how this cosmic dislocation played itself out in our daily lives. By doing this he emphasized the unrelenting challenge that evil presents to us. It never rests, and neither can we.

Dante Alghieri

The great Italian poet Dante Alghieri (1265–1321) wrote the epic poem *The Divine Comedy*. Dante was a Catholic, a Florentine, and a man well-versed in medieval theology. In *The Divine Comedy* the poet, or pilgrim as he calls himself, takes a fantastic journey through Hell into Purgatory and on up to Paradise. All three parts of the poem offer much for the discerning reader, but we are concerned with part one, Hell or, to use the proper title, *Inferno.* Much of the poem deals with contemporary Italian politics and can not be read today without a guide, usually provided by footnotes, but more of the poem has a timeless value as Dante shows us Evil in its own home.

This is an important point. We encounter evil on a daily basis in the world, in our home, yet Dante portrays evil in Hell, its proper home and thus in a place where evil is on display in all its fullness. When we enter the Inferno, we expect EVIL, but Dante gives it no power or majesty and certainly no glamour. The damned are in the Inferno forever, so their lives there are constant and unchanging, that is, absolute evil has become their daily life, and yet Dante shows evil not in its absolute but in its daily forms—petty, stupid, vicious, and vain.

But first we should see how Dante portrays the Inferno physically. When he wrote, people believed that the earth was at the center of the universe, and that the other planets, which included the sun and the moon, revolved around the earth in perfect circular spheres that became ever larger and wider as one moved out toward the realm of the stars (which were believed not to move) and to the creator God beyond them.

Since evil overturns the good, Dante's *Inferno* turned the heavens upside down. The heavens went upward, so hell goes down. The heavenly spheres became larger and wider, and so the hellish spheres became smaller and more narrow as one descended farther and farther down. As a journey through the celestial spheres led to God, so the journey through the infernal spheres led to Satan. God is warmth and light, but Satan is encased in darkness at the base of hell and, rather surprisingly, he is immersed in ice. Traditionally hell was a place of fire, but Dante put ice at the center to emphasize the coldness of eternal death. The devil's immersion in the ice meant that he could not move, and in medieval theology God represented perfect motion. God, as a perfect spirit, resides beyond the heavens, but the devil resides at the opposite end of the cosmos.

We all know that good and evil are opposites, but in this physical portrayal of the places where absolute good and absolute evil can be found, Dante gives an unforgettable image of this immeasurable gap.

This striking image also allows him to work other themes. We often imagine evil as the slippery slope. Once we start to go down that path, it is difficult to return. In his autobiography, *Inside the Third Reich*, Albert Speer, Adolf Hitler's armaments minister, recounts how he, as a young architect, gladly accepted commissions from the Nazis, believing that he would only have to design buildings and not have to go along with the party's ideology or practices. But he quickly found out that to keep his position, he had to look the other way once, then again, and then again, until finally he simply inured himself to what the Nazis were doing, finding out too late that he had slipped into their grasp and could not get out. This slippery slope even appears in modern fiction. Robert Bolt, an English playwright and atheist, genuinely admired Sir Thomas More, so much so that he wrote a great play about him, *A Man for All Seasons*. In a dramatic scene a young former employee of More is pressed by one of the king's agents to betray More in return for a sizeable bribe. The young man does not want to do this, but he eventually succumbs to the pressure and reluctantly turns on More. Seeing his distaste at the process, the king's agent assures him, "It will be easier the next time." It is.

Dante uses this idea to great effect. The deeper he goes into hell, not only do the imprisoned sinners become worse, for example, murderers are lower than adulterers, but Dante himself also becomes worse. The poet changes his language, making it increasingly more coarse and vulgar, and he also becomes more harsh. Early on, on the upper levels, he can be touched by the inmates' suffering, even to the point of fainting dead away, but as he goes farther below, he becomes inured to their plight and even takes on their characteristics. When he encounters an enemy of his family who is encased in ice up to his neck, Dante kicks the man in the head, a futile and malicious act. It is malicious because God has punished this man and does not need the poet's assistance, and it is futile because the man is in hell and thus beyond any suffering Dante can impose on him. Dante's imaginatively placing himself in this situation gives the slippery slope a stunning immediacy.

In the individual episodes Dante shows us "everyday" evil. At the top of the Inferno he meets people waiting transportation across the river Acheron into hell. He listens to their moans. They curse God, their parents, their country, their era, and the human condition in general. They never think to blame themselves.

On a lower level he meets the Gluttons, including Ciacco the Hog, who roots around in slime and dung, his gluttony having robbed him of his humanity. He meets the Misers and Spendthrifts, both burdened with huge weights which they use to crash against one another, withdraw, and repeat the process again for all eternity. Futility, mindlessness, revenge, and they can never rise above them. In a rare humorous note, Dante meets the Slothful, who, of course, do absolutely nothing for all eternity. They lie encased in muck, and air bubbles represent the only proof that they even exist.

The poet encounters the violent, the treacherous, the lecherous, and they all have the same trait—they never change, even though all their efforts and tricks will never change their situation. For me the most memorable of the damned are the Florentine nobles who ask Dante to mention their names to important people when he returns to the upper world. Amazing! They are in hell, and they still worry about their reputations. "Vanity of vanities, all is vanity."

As Dante reaches the base of hell, he knows he must get out, and he does, going from hell to purgatory. He is relieved, and so are we. This has been a difficult journey, but one that has shown us evil in its appalling diversity and baseness. If we see ourselves even partly reflected in Dante's characters, we would have a vivid picture of what evil does to us every day of our lives.

John Milton

The Englishman John Milton (1608–1674) was born to a middle-class London, Puritan family. After his blindness, he retired from public life to work on his poetry, finishing his masterpiece *Paradise Lost* in 1663. Milton knew Dante's work as well as that of the classical poets, and he wanted to write an epic poem on a monumental topic. He chose the Fall of Humanity.

The story of Adam and Eve occupies three chapters of the book of Genesis, about three pages in the average modern Bible. But Milton expands it one-hundredfold, adding a war in heaven between good and evil angels as well as a vision of the future that an angel gives to Adam before he and Eve must leave Eden. But the religious strength of the poem lies in its psychology of the characters, especially Satan, Eve, and Adam. Naturally Milton gives a long portrayal of God and his son Messiah, but they represent pure goodness and do not tell us about the nature of evil. Where Dante showed the petty venality of evil, Milton will emphasize its sheer self-delusion, a product of the unwillingness of his characters to face up to what evil is and what it has done to them.

Many religious people dislike *Paradise Lost* because of what they see as a majestic portrayal of Satan. But actually Milton is using the slippery slope. At the beginning of the poem, Satan has just fallen from heaven, and so he retains much of his angelic nobility. But as the story progresses and Satan becomes chronologically and, more importantly, spiritually distant from heaven, his majesty recedes and his viciousness comes to the fore. By the end of the poem he has become a serpent, slithering about the floor of hell. There are some scenes where Satan seems to be noble, as when he tells the other fallen angels that they can revenge themselves on God for expelling them from heaven (it was not, of course, *their* fault that they were expelled) by corrupting God's new little pets who live in some fantastic garden. Satan promises to fly across all the unfathomable depths that separate hell from earth and to encounter all the dangers involved. It sounds like Satan has courage, an admirable virtue, but he is actually moved by revenge. He is willing to face all these dangers in order to destroy two completely innocent people who have done no harm to him.

Some of Satan's supposed nobility appears in the memorable lines Milton gives him. At the beginning of the tale, when Satan rouses up his followers, he says, "The mind is its own place, and in itself / Can make a Heaven of Hell, a Hell of Heaven" (i.254–5). Magnificent words, to be sure, but basically Satan is saying that he will somehow convince himself that he is not really in hell. He simply cannot acknowledge what he has done to himself, so he will live in a world of delusion. A few lines later Satan announces that it is "Better to reign in Hell than serve in Heaven" (i.263). Nobly said, but completely absurd. How can ruling ever compensate for an eternity of filth, misery, frustration, and despair? Or is Satan one of those pathetic persons for whom being in charge is what counts, no matter what the misery for themselves or for others?

Satan's steady decline serves another purpose. Milton reminds us that although evil initially seems attractive—how much easier to cheat than to study, to criticize than to help—we find out as time goes by that evil exacts a terrible price from us in what it does to our personalities, which is just what Satan finds.

Satan's followers share his unreality. He assembles them and asks what they should do. One wants to battle God again in spite of knowing that they cannot win; another suggests that they wait in hope that God will change his mind, ignoring the obvious need for the demons first to repent for what they have done; a third suggests that if they accommodate themselves to hell, it might not seem so bad after a while. Satan's right-hand help Beelzebub dismisses these suggestions as "Hatching vain empires" (ii.378).

The fallen angels approve Satan's plan, and he flies off to earth. When he arrives in Eden, Milton brilliantly portrays an unspoiled paradise and how it appeared to someone from hell. "Beneath him with new wonder now he views, / To all delight of human sense exposed, / In a narrow room Nature's whole wealth, yea more / A Heaven on Earth" (iv.205–8). Satan realizes what his evil deeds have cost him. Eden is an "eternal Spring" (iv.268), constantly coming to life, but it does him no good. He has lost heaven and cannot enjoy this heaven on earth. But neither can he repent. He sees the goodness in front of him, he knows what he is missing, but he will not humble himself before his creator. His accursed pride will just not let him.

He soon spies Adam and Eve, "Godlike erect, with native honor clad / In naked majesty" (iv.289–90). Their nakedness indicates their unity with the natural world and the lack of shame before original sin. Satan realizes that he could love them, but his desire for revenge upon God soon wipes out any other thoughts. Taking the form of a serpent, he tempts Eve, using all kinds of devious arguments, even calling into question God's goodness. He suggests to Eve that God would not let humans eat the forbidden fruit because he wants to keep them ignorant so that he will remain in charge. Driven by dreams of grandeur, Eve ungratefully ignores all that God has done for her, and she eats the fruit. Milton here adds two brilliant details. First, he makes it clear that evil impacts not only us but the whole world around us. When Eve bites into the fruit, "Earth felt the wound, and Nature from her seat, / Sighing through all her works, gave signs of woe / That all was lost" (ix.782–84). Second, Eve did this as "the hour of noon drew on," that is, she sinned at noon, and God's Son would mount the cross at noon to save the world from what Adam and Eve had done.

In the biblical account, Adam takes the fruit immediately after Eve, which emphasizes that both disobeyed God. The gap between her and his eating the fruit is microscopic. But Milton expanded this gap, realizing that no matter how small it was, there was a time when one of the first human parents had sinned and the other had not, one had lost immortality and one still had a chance to keep it. Milton used this moment to show the workings of evil.

Eve thinks she has become like God, whom she contemptuously refers to as "Our great Forbidder, safe with all his spies (i.e., angels) / About him" (ix.815–16). She wants to let Adam know about her change . . . but, maybe not:

> *Shall I to him make known*
> *As yet my change, and give him to partake*
> *Full happiness with me, or rather not,*
> *But keep to the odds of knowledge in my power*
> *Without co-partner?*

Why?

> *so to add what wants*
> *In female sex, the more to draw his love,*
> *And render me more equal, and perhaps*
> *Superior—for inferior, who is free?* (ix.817–25).

This is a crucial passage. On the one hand, Milton supported patriarchy, showing Eve's (and thus women's) desire for equality to be a consequence of original sin; her desire to be superior went against the patriarchal view of the natural order. On the other hand, he knew that most women and probably many socially and economically oppressed men would relate to her desire for equality. Furthermore, Milton here gave Eve one of the poem's truly immortal lines: ". . . for inferior, who is free?" But the Puritan poet could venture just so far from his root values. Following the tradition that no human can do good from an evil base, Milton showed Eve's desires for equality degenerating immediately into something far inferior—jealousy:

> *but what if God have seen,*
> *And death ensue? Then I shall be no more,*
> *And Adam, wedded to another Eve,*
> *Shall live with her enjoying, I extinct* (ix.826–29).

Eve slides quickly down the slippery slope. She is actually jealous of someone ("another Eve") *who does not even exist.* Adam soon joins her in disobedience. His "loyalty" soon proves misplaced. After they both have the rush of "being like God," they soon find out they have been deluded and have deluded themselves. Furious, Adam blames everything on Eve; we are back in Dante's hell where no one is personally guilty of anything and other people are always at fault. But she turns back upon him, pointing out that even if he had been with her, the same thing could have happened; it could even have happened to him! She asks Adam, "Was I to have never parted from thy side? / As good have grown there still, a lifeless rib" (ix.1153–54). But Adam does not want to hear reason, and this book ends with the two hurling recriminations at one another. The two "gods" have become unhappy, bickering people.

As a Christian, Milton had a biblical sense of reconciliation. Adam and Eve finally accept their situation, and the archangel Michael foretells the redemption of humanity by the history of God's people Israel and by the death and resurrection of God's son Messiah. The poem even ends on a positive personal note for Adam and Eve who have become reconciled to one another: "They, hand in hand, with wandering steps and slow / Through Eden took their solitary way" (xii.648–49). But the title still applies: *Paradise Lost.*

Women Writers and the Faustian Theme

In late medieval Germany there circulated a legend about a scholar named Johann Faust who had sold his soul to the devil in return for knowledge that he could not gain in any human way. The devil granted him this knowledge but forced him to sign in blood a contract that he would deliver his soul over to the devil after a period of twenty-four years. Dr. Faust agreed, enjoyed the knowledge as well as the power that the devil gave him, but eventually paid the price.

This story became well-known to the English-speaking world through the Elizabethan drama *The Tragicall History of Doctor Faustus* by Christopher Marlowe (1564–1593), first performed in 1587. The Faustian story took on great popularity in Western culture, encouraging such significant literary works as *Faust: A Tragedy* by the great German poet Johann Wolfgang von Goethe (1749–1832), as well as musical works such the *Faust Symphony* by Hungarian composer Franz Liszt (1811–1886), and the opera *Faust* by French composer Charles Gounod (1818–1893). This attraction did not end with the nineteenth century. The twentieth-century Nobel-Prize-winning German author Thomas Mann (1875–1955) wrote a brilliant novel entitled simply *Doctor Faustus.*

But the Faustian tale that most of us know and which has earned remarkable popularity and endurance was a novel written by a nineteen-year-old woman named Mary Shelley (1797–1851). The book, of course, was *Frankenstein.* Although she is the first woman author we have cited, some people may consider Mary Shelley an odd choice for a religious book since she was a radical who notoriously scorned convention. Yet many religious women today find themselves being considered radical as they break new paths in the Church and society, so let us welcome Mary Shelley to this book.

Few books present a moral message so powerfully and so disturbingly as *Frankenstein.* The protagonist is Victor Frankenstein, a Swiss doctor who has a driving desire to create the perfect human being. He claims that he does not wish to do this for himself but rather for the betterment of the human race, although he loves the idea that he will become humanity's benefactor. He leaves home to study at a famous medical school. He becomes so involved with his studies that he ignores his family, neither visiting them nor even writing to them for years. In pursuit of his ambition, he literally cuts himself off from the people who love him. For Shelley, this becomes a terrible foreshadowing.

Victor creates his human being, his Adam, a man eight feet tall, larger even than God's creation, a symbol of what really motivates the scientist. But if Frankenstein has achieved knowledge previously held only by the divine, he soon learns that there is more to divinity than knowledge. His creation is huge but imperfect. It has yellow eyes and an overall frightening appearance. It repels Victor, who turns away from it. When the creature rises from the operating table and smiles at Victor, *as any baby would smile at his father,* Victor is appalled and runs away from his laboratory and returns home to his family, expecting that without him the creature will perish from neglect. Not only has Frankenstein failed as a god, he has failed as a parent. Shelley makes good use of the contrast with the Garden of Eden. Even after Adam and Eve sin and turn away from God, he continues to love them. Victor's innocent creation has done nothing wrong, and like all newborns it needs love, but this newborn's father denies that to him.

Victor realizes that his dreams have not come true, and he considers himself a failure, although at least he has escaped from the now dead creature. But Shelley wisely knew something that we do not like to admit. Our evil can spread to others, oftentimes without our knowledge and beyond our control. Victor thinks the matter is finished, that he has gotten away with his heinous deed, but, unexpectedly, the creature has managed to survive. Its hideous appearance causes people to attack it every time it seeks acceptance. In a moving scene, the creature sees its reflection in a pool of water and realizes why people want nothing to do with it, even though it is good. Outward appearance determines everything.

The creature wanders into a forest and comes across an impoverished family living in a hut. The mother is dead, and the blind father lives with his daughter Agatha and his son Felix. Mary Shelley has chosen the names carefully. Agatha means good in Greek and Felix means happy in Latin; these two young people can be good and happy, even in their wretched circumstances, because their father loves them, a sharp contrast to Victor. The creature watches the family and begins to help them, providing them with food to get through a harsh winter. He crouches beneath their window and hears their gratitude for the gifts this mysterious, unseen being has given them. Getting up his courage, the creature hopes that they will accept him, and he enters the house when the children are gone. In a very touching scene, the blind father, unable to see the externals, accepts the creature, seeing into the goodness of his heart, but, inevitably, when the children return, they are horrified and drive the creature away.

Considering this the final rejection, the creature despairs and now devotes itself to revenge, like Satan in *Paradise Lost*. It could kill Victor, but that would be too easy. The creature wants him to suffer as it has suffered, that is, by living a life without love. It methodically begins to kill the people whom Victor loves, exacting an apt but terrible retribution and simultaneously tumbling farther and farther down the slippery slope. Victor's *hubris,* his overweening pride, has returned to haunt him. To pursue his goal, he cut himself off from those who loved him. He now shudders in horror as the creature cuts them off from him forever.

For those readers who have not read *Frankenstein,* I will not recount any more of the story. It is a great book, and you will enjoy it more if you do not know how it ends. Let me just say that this terrible tale of pride, despair, and revenge portrays the consequences of playing God in a rare and almost devastating way. Like Adam and Eve, Victor wanted the knowledge only God could have, and like them he paid the price. And also like them, he watched in horror as his evil spread to innocent people.

Other nineteenth-century authors followed Mary Shelley's lead, showing the lengths people will go to for what they want, the prices they will pay, and the prices they will make others pay. In "Rappacini's Daughter," the American writer Nathaniel Hawthorne (1804–1864) portrays a scientist who creates his own Garden of Eden, filled with poisonous plants, in which he places his own daughter to be the new Eve and into which he lures a young student named Giovanni to be the new Adam. This Eden is no paradise but rather a hell. The Scottish author Robert Louis Stevenson (1850–1894) followed this path with his novella *The Strange Case of Doctor Jeckyll and Mr. Hyde.* Jeckyll, a brilliant physician, tries to remove the evil from human nature and transpose it into a purely evil being he called Edward Hyde, a play on words since evil is what we try to hide from the world. Like all Faustian figures, Jeckyll arrogantly assumes that he will always control his creation, only to find out that Hyde (=evil) turns out to be far more powerful than he had ever imagined; to his horror, he learns that evil is virtually unstoppable.

But these are all science fiction stores and thus put playing God in the realm of fantasy. Is there not a modern, realistic Faustian story? Yes, and by another woman writer. In 1962 the American Catholic author Flannery O'Connor (1925–1964) published a great short story, "The Lame Shall Enter First." It introduces us to Sheppard, a recent widower with a young son named Norton. Sheppard is a social worker who has devoted his life to helping society's underprivileged. On the surface, he is a good man who has done much for others, but he is a thorough-going secularist who believes that this world is all that there is and that good and evil are social constructs. If we can change society or overcome people's personal and social backgrounds, we can give them better lives—materially better since the spiritual world does not exist.

The boy Norton is distraught over his mother's death, but Sheppard, who should be a good shepherd, ignores his son's anguish in order to pursue his goal of creating a new human being. He plans to reform Rufus Johnson, an impoverished, homeless juvenile delinquent who suffers from a club foot. Frustrated with his efforts at the youth center, Sheppard decides to take Rufus (whose name means "red" in Latin) into his home, thinking that he can influence him more strongly in that environment but never considering what impact this will have on his son Norton. O'Connor had no use for secularist do-gooders, and she makes Sheppard's tragic flaw his faith in knowledge. If he knows enough, he can reform Rufus. But he never realizes that Rufus's problem is not his background. The problem is more fundamental: *Rufus is evil.* Sheppard cannot recognize it because he does not believe in it. Without *spiritual* redemption, Rufus cannot be helped.

O'Connor used a clever device that stretches far back into Christian history, actually to the fourth century when tales of the desert monks recounted their forcing the demons who harass them to tell the truth. Rufus knows who he is. He tells Sheppard, "The devil has me in his power," and he cunningly recognizes the truth about Sheppard. He tells Norton, "(Your father) thinks he's Jesus Christ." Sheppard's disbelief in evil guarantees that Rufus has no obstacle in perpetrating his evil on Norton and in repudiating all Sheppard's efforts to help him. The reformer bases everything upon a new shoe for Rufus's club foot, a special, medically engineered shoe that can help him to walk normally and thus fit into the larger world, Sheppard's definition of salvation. Rufus refuses to wear the shoe, symbolically refusing redemption.

As with *Frankenstein,* I do not wish to give away the end of the story to those readers who may want to read it themselves, but you can guess that Sheppard's world becomes a nightmare. A modern secularist cannot acknowledge the existence of evil and the need for spiritual redemption, and he pays a terrible price for his arrogance.

The Faustian story continues, even into our new millennium, for example, in the "Jurassic Park" movies which show an arrogant man who believes he can bring a lost world back to life, that is, to effect a resurrection of the dead, and always be able to control the situation. Indeed, Faustian stories will always be with us because we will always have the desire to play God, in minor ways by daily sin or in major ways like

Frankenstein and Sheppard. Faustian stories do not spring immediately to mind when we think of spiritual reading, but they give evil a vivid expression. In the hands of a strong believer and skilled writer like Flannery O'Connor, the Faust story can take on a religious dimension.

Reimaging a Biblical Book

Let me close with a modern scholar who is not well known outside professional circles and who offers a vivid picture of what evil does not just to individuals but to half the human race. At the 1990 meeting of the Catholic Biblical Association of America, Kathleen O'Connor gave a presentation entitled "A Feminist Hermeneutical Revision of the Book of Job." In it she reimaged this great biblical book with a woman protagonist, whom she called Joannah; O'Connor also changed the other human characters to women. In the biblical book the only woman with any role is Job's wife, who urges him to "Curse God and die" (2:9), and the man becomes the archetype of innocent suffering. But O'Connor wants to identify Joannah with women's suffering, not a major biblical theme, and she wants to see how a classic book on good and evil does not address evil as women often experience it. For example, the traditional idea of being rewarded for doing good and being punished for doing evil is here seen as a lack of mutuality between God and Joannah, reflecting the view of many women ethicists that relations between persons should be based primarily upon interaction and not upon regulations.

But O'Connor has stronger points to make. In the prologue, when Job accepts the hurt God allows Satan to visit upon him, he says nothing. When Joannah says nothing, O'Connor sees her "portrayed as a woman of complete passivity who recites rote prayers of submission, while everyone and everything dear is ripped from her . . . . Joannah is us." This recalls for O'Connor the time ". . . when our voices were not our own, when we were silent or spoke only in the words of the fathers, even as we ignored the pain and rage accumulating in our hearts." Even more: "The pain of women, in all its variety, parallels Joannah's. It is both physical and spiritual, external and internal. Joannah's loss of her children, honor, and wealth evokes the hunger, poverty, and homelessness of many women and their terror for their children. Her suffering conjures up illiterate and silenced women, women without political, economic, or religious voices, women who see their lives demeaned. . . ."

Recall that in the biblical book Satan also inflicts Job's body with sores. "Joannah's sores suggests the bruised bodies of battered, raped, and abandoned women . . . and of all of us who see the female body violated on the media. . . . These sufferings are not merely the generic miseries of the human condition, of the pathologies from which all humans suffer, they are the specific diminishments, indignities, and deaths that women know."

But, like the biblical Job, Joannah reaches salvation. ". . . her recognition of her own sufferings enables her to form new solidarities. . . . Her cries go beyond herself to incorporate the anguish of all sufferers as the world's pain rushes into her being. . . . What saves Joannah . . . is her honesty. She maintains her integrity despite every effort to wrest it from her. She will not live falsely with anyone. . . ."

The parallels between the story of Joannah and the book of Job are not exact. "What is missing from the Joannah story is the communities of women who have exchanged the truths of their lives, baptizing and confirming one another in the power of truth."

I regret to tell you that this paper has not been published because it should be read in its entirety. (My thanks to Professor O'Connor for permission to quote from it.) But the thrust of the paper is clear. The book of Job, which we will revisit in the next chapter, offers a classic picture of the problem of evil, but O'Connor demonstrates that it does not present evil as women have understood it over the millennia. She is right. If the biblical character were a woman instead of a man, we would read that book very differently.

We must thank these authors for the pictures of evil they have shown us, for the questions they have raised for us, and for the remarkable combination of imagination and clarity with which they have forced us to face the reality of evil.

This brief list hardly exhausts the possible readings. Many biblical books deal with evil, even little books like the Third Epistle of John, where we meet a Church leader who likes being in charge so much ("better to reign in hell . . .") that he abuses the early Christian obligation of hospitality. Augustine is the most prominent but hardly the only Church Father to write about evil, and to the Fathers can be added some of the great Medieval writers. The invention of the printing press guaranteed an ocean of books and, to maintain the metaphor, a sea of books on evil. In addition to "Rappacini's Daughter," Hawthorne depicted the evil of hypocrisy in his novel about a victimized woman in Puritan New England, *The Scarlet Letter,* while Joseph Conrad created an entire atmosphere of evil in *Heart of Darkness.* And no one can read *Night,* the account by Nobel Prize recipient Elie Wiesel about his experience of the Holocaust, or *One Day in the Life of Ivan Denisovich* by another Nobel Prize recipient, Alexander Solzhenitsyn, based upon his time in a Stalinist gulag, without being shocked at the ruthless efficiency of what are often seen as the ultimate modern evils.

Now we must see if there is any way we can reconcile the existence of God with this horrifying force.

Some Questions for Reflection and Discussion

1. This chapter provides a working definition of evil. How would you emend that definition?

2. We have seen that the "Wisdom of the Ages" can give us insights about evil. Are there other areas of Christian life where this wisdom can help? What makes an insight timeless?

3. Can you name some other biblical accounts other than Genesis 1–11 that cannot be taken literally but which contain valuable spiritual or moral messages?

4. Do modern Christians have difficulty accepting the true humanity of Jesus? Why?

5. Augustine said that sin separates us from the natural world, a gap that moderns want to bridge. As each living creature fills a niche in the ecosystem, what exactly is the niche of humanity? What responsibility does humanity have to the living planet? To what levels does this responsibility reach, for example, is it evil when we fail to conserve or recycle?

6. The "slippery slope" theory of evil says that the farther down we descend into evil, the more difficult it will be for us to climb back again. Is the reverse true, that is, does the higher we ascend into virtue make it more difficult for us to fall?

7. Adam and Eve, Victor Frankenstein, and Sheppard all wished to be like God and the result was evil. Is it always evil to want to be more than we are? What is the defining element that distinguishes hubris from normal ambition? Can we tell what it is to go too far before we have actually gone too far? Is human cloning the newest avenue to the slippery slope? If your answer is yes, then what would you say if someone compared cloning to things we take for granted today, such as airplane travel and heart transplants, that would have seemed like playing God to people of previous generations?

2

How Can God and Evil Coexist?

The Apostle Paul offers a model to all theologians and pastoral writers because he combined in his own person both theological brilliance and pastoral commitment. Unfortunately many later Christians see a division between the two, not in the sense that the two oppose each other but rather that they have little or nothing to do with one another. As a professor I must confess most of the problem lies with scholars who often do their work in almost willful ignorance of what is happening in the larger Church, and when that happens both scholar and Church pay the price, even when saints are involved.

In the late fourth century the great biblical scholar Jerome was asked by the pope to revise the existing versions of the Latin Bible, which were often poor translations. Jerome agreed, but soon found that he could not really revise the New Testament but had to translate it completely anew, which he did. He also did some translations of the Old Testament books. Toward the end of the fourth century, a priest in North Africa decided to use this new translation in a liturgy. When the people in the pews heard this new and, of course, unfamiliar version, they became angry, even infuriated that someone had tampered with the Bible. Word of this reached the most important North African Christian, Augustine, bishop of Hippo. He exchanged letters about this event with Jerome.

Augustine told him what had happened and how unfortunate it was that the new translation had caused difficulties, and he asked for his reaction. Jerome took the classic scholarly approach. He had done his translating accurately, so let the chips fall where they may. If his translation upset people, that was too bad for them. These ignoramuses had no right to impinge on his scholarly work. Augustine was an even greater scholar than Jerome and was sympathetic to scholarly work, but he was also a bishop who worked long and hard on his sermons, who took extensive and dangerous trips about a diocese that was increasingly threatened by barbarian invasions, and who dealt with all the minor everyday problems that any bishop faces. Augustine realized a central point that Jerome did not. Scholars do not own the Bible. The Bible belongs to the Church, to the whole people of God, and scholars cannot treat it as an ancient textbook that only they, with their specialized knowledge, can speak about.

Augustine did not favor inaccurate translations of the Bible, but he had the pastoral sense to realize that you cannot just shock people into something new. The old Latin translation had nourished the African church; it had formed the basis of the African liturgies; it was the Bible the African martyrs had quoted when the Romans arrested them and threw them into the arena. If it were inaccurate, it had to go eventually, but only after the congregations had been told why and had been introduced gradually to a new version.

As you have probably guessed, my sympathies lie with Augustine, and I am not alone in feeling that way. In his recent (2002) book on evil, *God, Evil, and Innocent Suffering,* American Catholic theologian John Thiel writes, "The academic environment in which theology has flourished can lead theologians to ignore the emotional lives of believers. This means that all good theology is pastoral theology" (p. 173). It would do a lot of us professors good "to get out more."

On the other hand, we do not want to overdo the "ivory tower" notion. As I once explained to a student who used that phrase, the grass in my lawn does not cut itself. Scholars have many of the same worries as those outside the academy, and evil would be at the top of most lists of concerns.

In this chapter I want to explain how Christian scholars try to reconcile the coexistence of God and Evil. In the next chapter we will consider some pastoral responses to evil.

The problem of reconciling God and evil can be put most succinctly this way:

> God is good and does not wish evil to exist.
> God is omnipotent and thus can prevent evil.
> Then why does evil exist?

This is actually more than just a problem, it is a mystery. Ironically, the word mystery itself is a problem. Christianity speaks routinely about mysteries, such as the mystery of the Trinity or the mystery of the Incarnation. Unfortunately, the English word mystery has the connotation of a puzzle that can be solved if only the information were available and we were intelligent enough to decipher it. If the brilliant television detectives have enough clues, they will figure out whodunit, and they always manage to do so in time for the final commercial. Lots of cable channels that specialize in nature or history offer programs like "The Mystery of the Pyramids." Unlike the detective programs, the scholars on these shows do not solve the mystery, but the viewer gets the impression that if some skilled archaeologist can discover and decipher some mummy's tomb or some wall inscription, the "mystery" will be solved.

As an avid reader of mystery novels, I will not criticize this meaning of the word, but it can be misleading for Christians. "Mystery" comes from the Greek word *mystérion* which means something that *cannot* be "solved." A mystery lies beyond our ability to comprehend it. The word appears very early in Christianity. Paul refers to the mystery of God in 1 Corinthians 2:1, while in Mark 4:11 Jesus refers to the *mystérion* of the kingdom of God. We cannot truly understand God nor can we understand the exact nature of his kingdom because they lie in the realm of the *supernatural,* another word that causes confusion in English.

We have all seen ads for television programs with names like "Tales of the Supernatural," and if you turn on such shows, you will not find a program about God or his kingdom, but rather you will hear eerie music and see a swamp covered in mist and, if you hang on a little longer, you will see some horrible monster emerge from the swamp and devour some unsuspecting teenager. Once again, we have to accept the common usage, but when the Church uses the word, it means "supernatural" in its basic Latin understanding of *super,* "above" or "beyond," and *natura,* "nature."

As a supernatural being, God is beyond human nature, beyond our capacity to understand, and as such he is a mystery. To be sure, we create images of God to help us envision a personal being, and we often make God look like ourselves with gender (male in Judaism and Christianity) and ethnic characteristics (European, African, Asian), but we realize that, in his essence, God is beyond our ability to understand.

Part of being a Christian is accepting mysteries, but that does not mean mindless acceptance. We must be people of faith, but not of "blind faith." That is a very offensive term because it implies that believers are mindless simpletons who swallow anything, no matter how absurd, if someone with ecclesiastical authority assures them it is so. This is patent nonsense. The Church does not want people to have blind faith. Look at the extensive educational establishment erected by the Church. Why have elementary schools, high schools, seminaries, colleges, and universities as well as catechetical and adult education programs if the Church wants only simpleminded believers?

The Church wants believers who want to know, and that is why the Church has always supported *theology,* a term best explained by the medieval scholar Anselm of Canterbury (1033–1109), who defined it as "faith seeking understanding." This is a wonderful definition, very economic and to the point. The theologian is a person of *faith* who is *seeking*, but not necessarily achieving, *understanding*. In many ways, *seeking* is the key word. Let me give two important examples.

We believe in the Trinity, that is, the Triune God. "Tri-" means three; "-une" means one. But how can there be three divine persons without there being three gods? To speak of three divine persons and one deity is contradictory, or at least it would be in human terms. Apprehending the Trinity can only be done by faith, but theologians at the first ecumenical councils in the fourth century created a Trinitarian theology, saying that the three divine persons share in the one divine substance. They gave a rational explanation, or, rather, they gave the best explanation they could, but they never claimed that because of their theology the Trinity ceased to be a mystery.

The same is true for the Incarnation. How can a person be both human and divine? Would not the human somehow lessen the divine? Would not the divine simply overwhelm the human? As with the Trinity, the Incarnation, in human terms, would be contradictory. But we apprehend it via faith, and at ecumenical councils in the fifth century, theologians created our basic Christology, understanding the Son of God to be one person with two natures, one human and one divine. As with those who created Trinitarian theology, these theologians did not claim that the Incarnation was no longer a mystery; rather they sought to understand what they knew in faith.

Bearing these examples in mind, we can approach the coexistence of God and evil as a mystery, and we can see what kind of approaches scholars have taken to that mystery. But there is one big difference. Many mysteries in Christianity seem remote from everyday life. We believe in the Trinity, but a mystery like the Trinity seems more a matter of the creed than of our daily lives. Evil, on the other hand, is a mystery that makes itself horribly present. We can easily picture ourselves or those we love caught up in Oklahoma City or September 11, people who went about their daily lives and were murdered for doing so. We read about crime in a mall where we shop. We ourselves may have been victims of some evil. This is why evil almost demands our attention, and it certainly demands the attention of believers who understandably wonder why God permits evil.

The attempt to reconcile the existence of God and Evil is called *theodicy*, from two Greek words meaning God *(theos)* and righteousness *(dike)*, and it was coined in the eighteenth century by a philosopher and Christian named Gottfried von Leibniz who, as we shall see, himself composed a challenging theodicy.

Relativism, Satan, the Other

We will first consider some theories that the Church has sensibly not used to explain the existence of evil.

One attempt to relieve God of the burden of allowing evil is a method widely rejected by most religious people but still used by some. This is *relativism,* the belief that there really are no such things as good and evil but rather it just depends upon how you look at something. What you think is evil someone else may think is good, and who are you to say that your view is correct and that person's is wrong?

Relativism is genuinely dangerous, but it grew out of some laudable attitudes. All of us have known people who know everything and do not hesitate to give us their views on our behavior, especially if they disagree with it. Of course, they do not know all the particulars, and we may not want them to know them. For example, you missed a committee meeting last night, and it was an important meeting since it dealt with attracting newcomers to some church activities. Worst of all, you offer no excuse for missing it. In fact, what happened is that you have a friend who is a recovering alcoholic or has just survived an abusive relationship. That friend needed you to be with her last night, but she does not want other people to know what she is going through, and you promised her to honor her request for privacy. You cannot tell anyone who is critical of you what really happened, and we can all see how easy it is for some know-it-all to make judgments based on ignorance.

We can escalate this attitude very easily. Many civilizations have been guilty of *ethnocentrism,* the belief that our group or our country or our civilization is superior to any other, and so we do not have to care what other peoples think or do. The history of North and South America proves how harmful that attitude can be. The European conquerors took it for granted that the native inhabitants were pagan savages whose cultures and civilizations had no value, especially in comparison with European ones. The conquerors bluntly assumed that the aboriginal peoples simply did not deserve to keep all this land but rather the land should belong to the superior Europeans. This attitude prevailed in much of the world besides the Americas, and too often Christianity was used to justify it. Native Hawaiians have a saying that "In the old days the white man had the Bible, and we had the land. Now we have the Bible, and the white man has the land."

Today we respect the right of all peoples to have their own values, even if we disagree with them. We do not wish to be cultural imperialists, imposing our culture's views on other cultures. But understanding and respect are good things and nowhere near relativism.

In a 1995 best-seller *Conversations with God: An Uncommon Dialogue,* the spiritual writer and counselor Neal Donald Walsch wrote that "'Right-

ness' or 'wrongness' is not an intrinsic condition, it is a subjective judgment in a personal value system. By your subjective judgments do you
create your Self—by your personal values do you determine and demonstrate Who You Are"(p. 48). *"Evil is that which you call* (his emphasis)
evil" (p. 61). There is even more: *"If there were such a thing as sin, this would
be it: to allow yourself to become what you are because of the experience of others"*
(his emphasis) (p. 62).

"Evil is that which you call evil." It certainly gets God off the hook, so
to speak, because if there is really no such thing as evil, and if evil is just a
name we apply to some act, then we do not have to reconcile God with
evil. But think of the consequences of this attitude. September 11 is not
evil if we do not call it evil. The Rwandan genocide is not evil if we do not
call it evil. Murder, lying, theft, and the whole panoply of things we think
are wrong will cease being wrong if we just stop calling them wrong. By
the way, the quotes I took from the book are in the mouth of "God," that
is, Mr. Walsch is claiming that God revealed these attitudes to him.

I live on the East Side of Cleveland, an area that has a large Jewish
population, including hundreds of Holocaust survivors, who by now are
very elderly and rapidly decreasing in number. I just wonder if Mr.
Walsch would go to a local synagogue and tell these survivors that the
Holocaust was not really evil, but rather "it just depends upon how you
look at it."

While I respect Walsch's right to express his views, I must say that no
Christian can take them seriously as a way to reconcile God and evil. To
abolish the notion of evil is to go against the experiences of our lifetimes
as well as against the very basis of Christian revelation. After all, if there
is really no such thing as evil, why did the Son of God become incarnate
and then suffer and die to redeem us from evil? Is his resurrection the
triumph over something nonexistent? And why, in that most famous of
all prayers, do we ask Our Father to deliver us from something that does
not exist?

Many readers may be surprised to see *Satan* listed among the theories
that the Church has passed over, but that is indeed the case. In a scientific age, many believers have trouble with the very notion of an evil
spirit, but Satan has a long and dishonorable history in Christian tradition and deserves inclusion in a discussion of evil. We include Satan
among the passed-over theories because in Christian tradition Satan
has never *caused* evil among humans, but rather he has *tempted* humans
to do evil. If Satan caused evil, he would be responsible for it, but the
humans who sin must take responsibility for their own actions. To be
sure, going about tempting people is an evil act, but all this means is
that Satan must take responsibility for his own actions. No evil spirit
causes us to sin. We can always resist temptation.

There is another, more important reason for excluding Satan from any theodicy. *Dualism* is the belief that there exist two divine principles, one good and one evil, and they battle forever to win over human souls. This theory eliminates the problem of why God does not use his omnipotence to eliminate evil. The good deity cannot do so because the evil one thwarts him, and he in turn thwarts the evil one. Christianity obviously centers around the belief in one God, and dualism is thus impossible, but some Christians elevate Satan's power to an almost dualistic level, seeing it as practically unlimited. We must always recall that Satan is not an evil deity with power equal to that of God. In Christian tradition, Satan is a fallen angel, a *created being,* and as such *under God's power.* As Scripture makes clear (Job 1–2), Satan acts in the world with God's permission. God could prevent Satan from tempting people, but he does not.

Theologians sum up the problem this way: if Satan does not exist, evil occurs *because God for some reason permits it;* if Satan does exist, he does his evil work *because God for some reason permits it.* The theological problem is divine permission of evil, not Satan, so there is no need to reconcile the coexistence of God and Satan but rather the coexistence of God and evil.

Let me emphasize that this does not prove that Satan does not exist, but only that Satan is not a central problem in modern theodicy.

The theory of the *Other* repulses every modern Christian. Basically this theory blames evil in the world on some group, often an entire race of people or even a gender, which dedicates itself to working against Christ and his Church. This is prejudice, pure and simple, and it has no validity today. Unfortunately, for too long in Christian history people did blame the Other, for example, heretics in the Middle Ages and "witches" in the seventeenth century. The deepest and most persistent attack on the Other has been anti-Semitism, evident as early as the first century and growing more virulent through the centuries, culminating in the twentieth century with the Holocaust. Modern Christians recognize the unbelievable harm this "theory" has done, and they reject it. In a dramatic gesture, Pope John Paul II apologized for the harm Catholics had done to Jews during a visit to Israel in 2001. Loathing the Other has hardly disappeared as ethnic and racial violence prove, but it no longer has any value as an explanation for evil.

Now that we have taken a brief look at some well-known but erroneous and even harmful explanations for the coexistence of God and Evil, let us turn to some of the more plausible ones.

Original Sin

This theory is well known because it derives from the story of Adam and Eve in the Garden of Eden in the opening chapters of the book of Genesis, right? Well, not exactly. The Bible never uses the phrase "original sin," not in Genesis nor in the Epistle to the Romans where Paul speaks of Adam's bringing death into the world. As we saw in the first chapter, the African theologian Augustine of Hippo first used the phrase "original sin" in 393. Augustine believed that when Adam and Eve disobeyed God, they not only sinned but they broke the bounds between humans and nature; furthermore, they corrupted human nature so severely that we are literally born damned to hell and we can do nothing good on our own. He also believed that baptism could remove the guilt of original sin so that we have a chance for salvation, but he was quite willing to send hordes of unbaptized pagans and Jews to damnation. Baptism might remove the guilt of original sin, yet we still have the tendency to sin. We cannot overcome it, but God can give us grace, which we can do nothing to earn, to help us overcome the power of sin. Of course, God does not *have* to give grace to anyone. Rather, before the creation, he chose those whom he would save, a theory known as predestination. Augustine did not think that God chose to save many people, and many other Christian thinkers followed him in this, for example, the great Protestant reformer John Calvin with his belief in the total depravity of unbaptized humans.

This famous theory has always presented difficulties for believers. It seems so horribly unfair that because two prehistoric people took a bite out a piece of fruit that all of humanity is condemned to hell or that God seems to act capriciously in deciding whom to save and whom to damn. The theory's most formidable difficulty today is that it rests heavily, almost completely, upon the actual historical existence of Adam and Eve. Since the rise of modern geology and evolutionary biology in the nineteenth century as well as the great advances made by scriptural scholars in deciphering and understanding other ancient Near Eastern literature with stories similar to those in Genesis, modern Christians, except for fundamentalists, do not consider the Garden of Eden account to be historical.

For example, Augustine believed that carnivorous animals did not eat meat in the Garden of Eden. He could not figure out how a lion fed itself, but he knew that it did not devour the lamb. Being carnivorous came about as a consequence of Adam and Eve's sin. But evolution has demonstrated that animals have always preyed upon one another and did so eons before humans even existed.

But if the classic notion of inherited guilt carries no weight today, does that mean that the Church has abandoned the notion of original

sin? Not at all, but theologians now have to redefine it so that it pre-
serves its biblical foundation but also has relevance in the modern era.

A good and concise example of how modern theologians interpret
original sin is an article on the topic by Fr. Sean Fagan in *The Modern
Catholic Encyclopedia.* He writes,

> To make it (the doctrine of original sin) meaningful and credible in
> today's scientific culture, theologians have attempted to distinguish
> between the substance of the teaching and its formulation, that is,
> Augustine's view of the Garden of Eden, with the reminder that the
> latter of necessity will be culturally conditioned (that is, he consid-
> ered the garden to be a physical one). It would seem that the sub-
> stance of Christian faith in this area can be summarized in the
> statements: that Christ is at the very center of the divine plan, that all
> human beings have a basic need of the redemption he brought about,
> and this need is antecedent to any act of sin on their part, or even
> mere exposure to a sinful environment. . . . Genesis 3 is not a literal
> description of an historical first sin, but an ingenious psychological
> description of all sin. . . . (Original sin) stresses the flawed state of
> our basically good human nature as intended and created by God,
> and sets that in the context of Christ's saving grace (p. 621).

What an insightful and encouraging interpretation. Human nature is
essentially good but flawed and thus in need of redemption. I say that it
is an insightful interpretation because it meets not just theological but
psychological needs. We know we are not fundamentally evil people. If
we were, we would not care about doing good. But we also know that
we sin; our essentially good nature is not without flaws.

Modern interpretations of original sin do not overlook the negative
but stress the Christocentric positive. To quote Father Fagan again,

> The doctrine of original sin is a foil to proclaim that where sin abounds,
> grace does more abound, that in Christ there is the *fullness of forgiveness
> and healing.* Indeed, recent theology extends the work of Christ beyond
> the human family to embrace the whole of creation, echoing St. Paul's
> words about "nature groaning for its salvation" (p. 622).

Notice that Father Fagan speaks of God embracing "the whole of creation," thus negating the predestinationist view of God coldly choosing
one person while abandoning another.

Unlike Augustine and some medieval theologians, ever so eager to de-
port hordes of pagans and Jews and heretics and sinful Christians to
hell, the modern Church insists not only on the reality of evil but also
on God's wish to save us all and the work God's Son has done to bring
about that salvation.

Divine Nature and Human Free Will

Many Christians have wondered whether God could have created us in such a way that we would not sin. After all, he does have unlimited power. Several atheistic critics of Christianity have used the same argument to claim that evil proves that God does not exist because a good and powerful God would not permit evil.

Many great Christian thinkers have written in opposition to that claim, and their arguments revolve not around trying to prove anything about evil so much as to understand the nature of God.

When we say God is omnipotent, we usually mean that he can do absolutely anything, but when we say that, we are wrong. (Please keep reading. I am not a heretic!) For example, can God create a four-sided triangle? No, because by definition a triangle has three sides, so there can never be a four-sided triangle. More to the point, can God sin? This is a particularly interesting question because we can sin. Does this mean that we can do something that God cannot? Do we have a power that God does not?

In response, theologians point out that God must act in accordance with his nature, that is, he must act like God. It seems a bit odd to say that God **must** do something, but that really is the unavoidable conclusion. If not, that means that God can act in a way contrary to his own divinity, and how can that be? Sinning would be a serious defect in God, not proof of one more thing that he can do. Let us use a human parallel. Parental abuse of children has become a serious problem in modern society. It is always sad when any child is abused by anyone, but we consider it worse when the perpetrator is a parent. Why? Because parents, *by virtue of being parents,* have the task of raising a child, protecting the child, training him or her to be a good person, and, most important of all, loving the child. When a parent abuses a child, the parent goes against what it is to be a parent. Parents are just not supposed to abuse children. Period. No discussion. Abuse does not demonstrate the range of the parent's powers but rather contradicts the essence of what it means to be a parent. Thus, when we say that God cannot sin, we mean simply that an all-good being whose gracious providence guides the world must act like God. To sin is impossible for God.

When Christian theologians apply this to the problem of evil, they reason that God, who made us in his image and likeness (Gen 1:26-27), had to make us created beings *worthy of himself.* Could God have created us so that we could never have sinned? Theoretically, yes, but then he would have created moral robots, automatons incapable of making moral decisions. But how can beings like that bear the divine image and likeness? God had to make beings worthy of his image and likeness, and that meant that he had to give them intellect (God knows) and will (God loves). God knows that our intellects are fallible and will make mistakes; he also knows that our wills are fallible and will also make mistakes, that is, we will sin. *But it is better for us to have free wills, to be in the image and likeness of the divine, and to make moral decisions, even wrong ones, than to be moral robots.*

Let me use another analogy, once again using children. It is possible for parents to form children who will never disobey their parents. This can be done by a combination of discipline, intimidation, and brutality so that we form children who are literally terrified to think for themselves. They obey us because they fear the consequences of not doing so. Some parents do that, and I suppose to them it seems easier and more effective than sitting down with a child and trying to explain why people should do what is right because it is right. ("O.K., I understand that you think she's making a big deal out of nothing, but how would you feel if she used your toys without asking you first? Wouldn't you be annoyed?") But all sensible people would agree that we have to help children to form their consciences and to learn how to make moral judgments, to do what is right because it is right and not because they are petrified of what punishment they will suffer if they do not follow exactly what their parents have told them to do.

One of the most famous promoters of the theory of moral autonomy is the Christian who invented the term *theodicy,* Gottfried Wilhelm Baron von Leibniz (1646–1716). He said that God created this, *the best of all possible worlds.* This famous phrase lies open to much misinterpretation. The French writer Voltaire (1694–1778) parodied it in his novella *Candide,* where the characters undergo a seemingly endless list of disasters, which they refuse to see as disasters because this is the best of all possible worlds. At the other end of the pendulum, some religious people have turned this into platitudes like "It's all for the best" or "It's God's will," whenever anything terrible happens.

These two platitudes assume that we cannot understand the divine mind (which is true), so therefore any evil, no matter how terrible, must be part of a divine plan (which is false). Over the centuries Christian thinkers have acknowledged that God *permits evil,* but that is a far cry from God's *deliberately including evil* in some plan for the cosmos. As we have just seen, God can do only good, so he *does not and cannot* include evil in his designs. Using evil would go against everything God is. He abhors evil. For God, evil can never be "for the best," nor does God will evil. In fact, even the people who use these phrases probably do not really believe them because it is one thing to say it to themselves or among people who have not suffered evil but something else to apply it to a particular evil situation. Suppose we knew the parents of a child who had been kidnapped and murdered. Could we really go to them and say, "It's all for the best"? It is loathsome to even think about doing such a thing. The parents would find that remark insensitive to the point of cruelty, and it would be incredulous that anyone could say something like that. I cannot believe any Christian would do something like this, but if someone really believes that "It's all for the best," why would he or she not say that to the parents? After all, would that not "comfort" them? The same is true for "It's God's will." What kind of God would will the kidnapping and murder of a child? And, once again, would we—could we—say something like that to the child's parents?

When Leibniz said that this is the best of all possible worlds, he was confirming something that all believers know. God cannot do a second-rate job. How could he not create the best of all possible worlds? But this world has evil in it, and we can easily conceive of a world without evil (obviously we are not including here a heavenly afterlife in which evil is an impossibility). But Leibniz pointed out that this is not the best of all *conceivable* worlds but the best of all *possible* ones. After all, if we can think of a better world than this, so can God. If he chose not to create the world that we can think of, then he must have had a reason, one which we cannot comprehend. God always does good, so if he created this world, he knew that it was the best possible one, even if not the best conceivable one. This world contains evil but no more than is consistent with its being the best of all possible worlds.

There is another cautionary note here. Just because we can conceive of a better world does not mean that such a world is indeed better. We should recall the ancient Greek myth of Midas, a powerful and wealthy king who had so much but who, like Adam and Eve, like the Faustian characters, wanted so much more. When a god offered Midas the chance to have whatever he wished for, Midas promptly requested that everything he touched would turn to gold, thereby increasing his wealth beyond his dreams. (This is where the phrase "the Midas touch" comes from.) Delighted by his new power, Midas went about the palace, turning tables and chairs and vases into pure gold. The king was living in the best world he could conceive of. But transforming things into gold proved to be exhausting work, and Midas decided to relax and have some lunch. He quickly found out that he could not eat golden food or drink golden wine. *Everything* he touched became gold. The distraught Midas sat and wept at what he had done to himself. Seeing him weeping, his young daughter went to him to comfort him. Without thinking, the king embraced her, only to find himself hugging a golden statue. Almost despairing, he asked the god to take back the terrible gift; fortunately for him, the god did so, and his daughter was restored to life.

We simply cannot be sure that what we conceive to be a better world is necessarily so. Like Leibniz, believers have to trust to God's providence that this world, with all its faults, is the best of all possible worlds because God would not do a second-rate job. We must also realize that evil exists in this world because of us, not God. He gave us a gift, free will, but we are the ones who have to use it for the good. If we did not have it, we would be moral robots. As Leibniz put it, "To wish that God should not give free will to rational creatures is to wish that there be none of those creatures" (*Theodicy* 119.iv).

The modern, technical term for this approach is the *Free Will Defense,* and modern scholars naturally use different terms and forms of argumentation than Leibniz did, but the basic principle remains the same. God must act like God. He must create creatures worthy of himself. To create beings in his own image and likeness means that he has given those creatures intellect and will. If he did not, those creatures would be unworthy of God. God does not wish us to do evil, but he knows that giving us free will gives us the possibility to do so, but it is better for us to have free will with the possibility of doing evil than for us not to have free will at all.

Like a good human parent, God knows that his children will often let him down, but he also knows that they will listen to him most of the time and do good far more often than evil. After all, look at the people we admire—Mahatma Gandhi, the Reverend Doctor Martin Luther King, Jr., Mother Theresa of Calcutta—people who changed the world for the better by their work and example. We want to do good, even if we often fail, and God knows that. Our Father forgives us, expects us to do better the next time, will understand when we fail again, and will take parental pride when we use his precious gift of free will to do good. Furthermore, like a good parent, God will help us as he has already via the Scriptures, the Church, and, most importantly, the Incarnation of his Son. God does not just give us free will and wish us "Good luck." His grace, if we accept it, can help our fallible wills to choose good.

"Are You Glad You Exist?"

Christian thinkers were able to demonstrate that the value of our having a free will negates the notion that the coexistence of God and evil is logically impossible and that the existence of evil means that God cannot exist. But some atheist thinkers took the argument a step further, questioning God's existence by emphasizing gratuitous evil.

The term "gratuitous evil" means an evil event from which no good can come or, as believers would put, evil from which God can bring no good. This is a powerful argument because one way in which believers can reconcile God and evil is by pointing out that God can bring good from evil events. This does not mean that the evil event is any less evil, but rather that God's providence does not abandon us and that he can find some way to give the event some meaning.

This is very evident at the Oklahoma City Memorial to those who were killed in the 1995 bombing. Significantly, the memorial contains not a hint of retribution or righteous wrath against the perpetrator. All the emphasis falls upon two things: what happened and how to move on. The memorial shines with simplicity. The bomb went off at 9:02 a.m. You enter the outdoor memorial through a rectangular wall with a door in it. As you look up, you see the time 9:01 in large numbers, the last moment of life for 167 people and the last moment of innocence for many more. Ahead of you is a shallow reflecting pool and on a grassy rise to the left are 167 chairs, 162 representing the people in the building who were killed and the remaining five for the people on the street who also were killed. The chairs are arranged according to "floors" so that each row of chairs represents the number of people on a particular floor who died. The nursery was on the second floor, and so the second row has a sad line of small chairs. Each chair has a victim's name on it. The empty chairs have a great effect on the visitor. These people went to work and were murdered for doing so. Any one of us could have been any one of them. When you look at the empty chairs, you realize that, and the impact of that realization can be devastating. As you walk past the chairs, you head toward another rectangular wall with a door in it, and above this door, in numbers the size of those on the first wall, you read 9:03, the time when the healing and reconciliation began.

The Oklahoma City Memorial is a truly stunning monument, very difficult to visit but impossible to stay away from. My wife and I visited it on our first day in Oklahoma City, and we felt compelled to visit it again just before we left. As a public monument, it is naturally a secular one, but it produces a spiritual feeling that eludes so many famous, gaudy religious shrines. The open and clear emphasis on healing and reconciliation tells every visitor that although a horrendous evil was done here, evil will not ultimately triumph.

Just across the street is a smaller memorial. St. Joseph's Old Cathedral, a Catholic church, has in its yard an almost overpowering statue of Jesus entitled "And Jesus Wept," a citation of John 11:35. The statue portrays Jesus wretched, distraught, and broken down in tears, a stunning portrait of the Son of God sharing his humanity with all the other visitors to the site. This, too, has great impact on the visitor.

Not all evil events from which good can arise need be so monstrous. In fact, most are everyday events. Suppose a white woman has a black friend, and the two of them go shopping together. The white woman is a good Christian person who opposes racism, but who has done so only in a general, intellectualized way. Yet when she goes into the store and watches the store clerk's eyes follow her friend everywhere and then sees the clerk "casually" stroll around the store and just "accidentally" happen to be no more than ten feet from her black friend the whole time, this white woman now sees racism not as a notion to be discussed and opposed in principle but as the vicious little humiliating acts that black people must endure every day. The immediacy of this personal experience has changed this white woman forever. She now has a deep commitment to equality and the will to make her society a fairer one to all people.

But atheist critics attack this notion along two lines. First, can God ever bring enough good out of evils like the Holocaust or the Rwandan genocide or September 11 to make those events less monstrous? The believer replies that this is not a matter of spiritual bookkeeping. When religious people say that God can bring good out of evil, they *never* claim that this makes the evil any less monstrous. They also *never* claim that God intended to work through this evil. God did not want the Holocaust or the Rwandan genocide or September 11 to happen. God does not will evil and, like the Jesus portrayed in the Oklahoma City statue, laments when his creatures do evil. All believers claim is that no event can be so evil that it excludes God's providence.

Let me give an example. Like teachers all over the United States, I discussed September 11 with my students. I made it clear to them that the event was thoroughly evil, but then I asked them if any good could come from it. They had several suggestions, but many emphasized the laudable reaction of the American government and people in working to keep Arab-Americans and Muslim-Americans from becoming the victims of persecution the way that Japanese-Americans were during World War II. Several commented about how Americans often act if the words "Arab" or "Muslim" are prefixes before the word "terrorist." We often did nothing about prejudice against our fellow citizens as well as against people who, like Jews and Christians, are Children of Abraham.

The students' responses delighted me, but I had to point out that we—and I emphasized that this included me—should have been conscious of these attitudes long before September 11. We should not have needed so horrible an event to shake us out of our prejudices. And this is the approach we should take to bringing good out of evil. That we have now brought that good into being is important, but *we have to take the responsibility for not bringing that good into being before the evil occurred.* The evil did not produce the good; it forced us to recognize an evil so that we could turn to a good to combat it. God does not want to bring good out of evil because God does not want evil to happen. Yet when it does happen, he helps us to bring something from it.

Yet atheistic critics return with another attack. If religious people insist that God can bring good out of evil, then they cannot ever admit that there is a purely gratuitous evil because if they do, they would have to admit a weakness on God's part—here is an evil event from which he could not bring good—and that would destroy the theists' belief in God.

This argument has some merit. We share the earth with over five billion people, and all of us manage to do something wrong every day. That is a lot of evil acts for God to bring good out of, critics say. Granted, believers can always say that there is a divine plan that we cannot fathom, but critics would scorn this as just a catch-all excuse. Must there not be some gratuitous evils, they would say, some evils from which God cannot bring a good? This is a difficult one for believers who, after all, must insist that God's providence cares for every one of his creatures, and they must also insist that there is no limit to the evils that providence can deal with. It is easy to see how critics could focus in on this apparent weakness in the theist explanation of evil.

But some recent writers have suggested an important and almost ingenious answer by asking the question, "Are you glad that you exist?" Not, "are you happy?" or "do you have no wants?" but are you glad that you simply exist, that you just are? As the originator of the theory, William Hasker, suggests, there are presumably only a handful of people who would answer no to that question.

But if you are glad that you exist, you must look at those forces that brought you into existence. Initially you might find nothing but good forces, such as your parents meeting one another while on a summer job. But, if you keep digging, you will find, somewhere, somehow, that evil intervened. As an American, I can offer an obvious example. With the exception of Native Americans, all Americans take their descent from immigrants, people who came to this country from abroad and who usually did not wish to do so. They came to this country fleeing poverty or oppression or ethnic hatred; many came as political refugees; many came as slaves. I, my wife, our parents, our siblings, our children, our grandchildren, and, I suspect, most if not all readers of this book are in existence because our ancestors endured evils.

And thus the dilemma. We clearly do not rejoice in our ancestors' sufferings. As human beings, we wish that they did not have to suffer. Yet at the same time, we know that if they had not encountered evil, we would not be here discussing this topic—indeed, we would not be here doing anything. We are glad that we and those whom we love exist, but we must acknowledge that we are able to do so because of an evil. *There is no way we can be glad about their suffering.* As a person of Irish descent, I could never say that I am glad that the Famine of 1846–1849 occurred and drove my ancestors to North America, yet my siblings and I and our families would not be in existence if the famine had not occurred. Since we are glad that we exist, since our existence is something good, it is thus possible that some good does indeed come from every evil.

If using our ancestors' sufferings is too broad a canvas, let us put the question on an individual level. Two young people are deeply in love and engaged to be married. The woman goes to the bank to deposit some money in her account because she is saving up to furnish their new apartment. Unfortunately for her, she is in the wrong place at the wrong time. A couple of armed thugs arrive to rob the bank. The security guard attempts to stop them, and shooting breaks out. A stray bullet hits the young woman and kills her.

Her fiancé is absolutely devastated and can see no future for himself. But family, friends, and faith help him to get through a very difficult period, and he eventually is able to get on with his life. He meets someone else, they get married, and they have three children. This man deeply loves his wife and he adores his children. Yet he knows that he would not have met this woman and his children would never have existed—literally would not have existed—if his first fiancée had not been murdered. Clearly he cannot actually be glad that she encountered such vicious evil, but just as clearly he cannot wish that his children did not exist. Her tragic death remains an evil event, but one from which God has been able to bring about some good.

Critics will surely not cease to use gratuitous evil to argue against the existence of God, and just as surely, believers will wonder what good came or could possibly come from this-or-that evil, but given the interconnectedness of creation, we can be certain that somehow God will find a way to bring some good from any evil, even if the victims of that evil, like our ancestors, do not have the opportunity to recognize that good.

A Changeable and Nonomnipotent God?

In 1981 Rabbi Harold Kushner published an important book, *When Bad Things Happen to Good People.* Its publisher called it a book "For Anyone Who Has Been Hurt by Life." The publisher's blurb did not exaggerate.

Rabbi Kushner had a son named Aaron. As he tells it, "My wife and I had been concerned about his health from the time he stopped gaining weight at the age of eight months, and from the time his hair started falling out after he turned one year old." When Aaron was three, the Kushners took him to a pediatric research specialist who told them that their son suffered from a rare disease called progeria or "rapid aging."

This meant that "Aaron would never grow much beyond three feet in height, would have no hair on his head or body, would look like a little old man when he was still a child, and would die in his early teens." Faced with this situation, Kushner "could only repeat over and over again in (his) mind, 'This can't be happening. It is not how the world is supposed to work'" (pp. 1–3).

A sensitive man faced with a tragedy, Kushner knew he would some-day write a book about his ordeal but only after his son's death, which occurred two days after the boy's fourteenth birthday. As a rabbi, Kushner knew the story of Job and other teachings about suffering; as a Jew, he knew of the horrors visited upon his people; as a religious person, he wondered how God could allow such suffering.

He came to a conclusion that may surprise many people, but which has actually been around for a while. He concluded that God is not omnipotent, that is, that God's power has limits. This in turn means that God does permit evil or suffering not because he chooses to but be-cause he *cannot* prevent them. A group of theologians, called process theologians, had reached that conclusion well before Kushner did, but the rabbi's book put the idea in front of a mass audience. Interestingly, most process theologians are Catholics or mainline Protestants, not Jews.

Process theology involves some intricate and difficult argumentation, but here we will just summarize its more important conclusions for our understanding of evil. Some critics have accused process theologians of being afraid to face the paradoxical consequences of evil, namely, that an all-good and all-powerful deity does not stop evil, and they do this by getting rid of divine omnipotence, thus, in effect, "getting God off the hook" by saying that he lacks the power to abolish evil. But that is not the case.

Process theologians see God growing and changing with the cosmos. That in itself presents a problem for people who have been taught that God cannot change. This teaching grows out of the notion of divine per-fection. If God is perfect, he can only change for the worse, and so it is impossible for him to change. It is rather like a student getting 100 per-cent on an examination and asking to take it again in order to get a bet-ter grade. The student cannot do better; the only change in the grade would be for the worse. God's immutability does not appear in the Bible but was theorized during the early centuries of Christian history.

God's immutability runs into problems of its own, including that of petitionary prayer. We pray to God to ask him to do something for us. Whether he does so or not (the answer to many prayers is no), we would not pray unless we believe that our prayers can affect God in such a way that our prayers would be granted. But even more fundamentally, divine immutability runs into biblical problems. In Genesis, God regrets that he had made the human race and so sends the Great Flood. In 2 Samuel 24, God sends an avenging angel to destroy Jerusalem but then changes his mind. One could claim that Genesis is a myth and 2 Samuel repeats a legend, but the point is that much biblical teaching shows a deity who changes.

More importantly, the Bible teaches that God loves us, a simple phrase we hear constantly, but one that has great consequence for how God deals with us. When we love people, we do not use power with them. When a problem arises, we listen first to what they have to say, then we talk to them and try to help them to see our point of view, and throughout the whole time we emphasize that the love that binds us means far more than the problem that separates us. Maybe an exercise in power would "solve" the problem in the sense that what we want done got done, but what good is a "solution" which damages a loving relationship? It would help to remember here how the Son of God chose to deal with problems when he was on earth. In Matthew's Gospel (26:53), he tells the disciple who wants to use weapons to defend him from arrest, "Do you think that I cannot appeal to my Father, and he will at once send me more than twelve legions of angels?" Jesus submitted to arrest, and he went on to save the world through suffering, not omnipotence.

To be sure, there are many places in the Old Testament where God uses brute force (the ten plagues), and the Christian book of Revelation revels in displays of divine power. The point here is that it is not unbiblical to picture a loving God acting in an other-than-omnipotent way.

But the notion of a loving God carries even more weight with it; it implies a God who can change. When we love others, we become vulnerable. They can hurt us by things they say or do, as, of course, we can hurt them. Coarse or thoughtless actions do not necessarily destroy a relationship, but they do make us wonder why people do such things and how we can be reconciled to them. Love brings a unique joy, but sorrow can sometimes follow in its train. *When we say that God loves us, we are also saying that we can hurt God by our actions.* How can someone who loves us not be disappointed when we let him down? When we say something harsh to someone or when we keep quiet when someone needed us to speak up for him or her, God feels the effects of our actions. When we help the poor and comfort the bereaved, God is warmed by the love we show his creatures. *An unchanging God could not be affected by what we do, but a loving God is always affected by what we do.* To return to that statue "And Jesus Wept" in Oklahoma City, the sculptor portrayed Jesus not serenely above and beyond all the suffering but rather weeping at the harm done to those whom he loved.

For some theologians, a nonomnipotent God is not a weak deity but a good one who does not threaten but rather tries to win us over with love. God sees the choices we face, and he somehow encourages, not forces, us to make the moral one. Sometimes we do, sometimes we do not. Yet God will not use his power to make us do good, although he will suffer disappointment when we choose evil over good. Every evil act is a tragedy, but God helps us to understand the harm of evil and shares the pain that evil causes. In the words of the founder of process theology, Alfred North Whitehead (1861–1947), God is "the fellow-sufferer who understands."

The notion of a God who is not omnipotent presents many problems, going, as it does, against two millennia of Christian tradition, and the question is far from settled. But every generation of the Church contributed to the building of Christian tradition, and who can say now what our generation will contribute?

Let us close this section by returning to Rabbi Kushner. In preparing his book, he read, conferred, and thought a great deal, and when he had finished, he had a better understanding of evil and one that he could share with others. But, he frankly admits, he would trade in all that knowledge to have his son still alive. Theories may explain suffering, but they do not take it away.

"Who is this who darkens counsel by word without knowledge?" *God's Incomprehensibility*

The quotation comes from the book of Job 38:2, when that tortured, unhappy man finally gets his wish that God will tell him why he has suffered so. This book also provides support for the traditional Christian explanation of the coexistence of Evil and an omnipotent God.

Job is one of the Bible's great books. Written by a now anonymous Jew, most likely in the sixth century B.C.E., it represents the universalist strain in ancient Judaism, a biblical book that deals not just with problems relating to God and Israel but with a problem all people face at some time: innocent suffering. (The universalist strain also appears in the character of Job who is a Bedouin Arab, a non-Jew and yet the model for a righteous man.)

For Jewish traditionalists, if people suffered, it was because of some evil that they had done. In this all-encompassing theory, innocent people simply did not suffer. The anonymous author of Job found this explanation too facile, and he faced up to the question of innocent suffering. He used his considerable skills to frame the issue in a way the conservative religious mind could accept while still making a daunting rejection of the accepted view.

The prologue set in heaven introduces the story. Satan, one of the heavenly court, has been traveling on earth. God asks him if he has seen God's servant Job, a righteous man. Satan claims that if God were to take away what he had given Job, this righteous man would curse him to his face. God permits Satan to test Job, which he does with horrible consequences, killing all of Job's children and destroying his sources of wealth. But in spite of this Job does not curse God. Not deterred by Job's faith, Satan claims that if Job's body suffered, he would give in. God again gives Satan permission to test Job; this time he covers his body with sores, but Job still does not curse God.

This prologue establishes the folkloric nature of the tale. By the time Job was written, the Jewish understanding of God had moved well beyond the stage where he had to accept Satan's challenge. All God really had to do was tell Satan that he was wrong and that would be the end of the matter. But the folkloric setting meets an important goal of the author. It enabled the traditionalist to read an account which acknowledged innocent suffering, because it is, after all, just a story and need not be taken too seriously. The ending of the book reinforced this because there God gives Job more children and more wealth. The shortsighted reader could actually finish the book thinking that nothing had really changed, that Job certainly suffered but God made it up to him and even gave him more. Yet between the prologue (ch. 1–2) and the ending (ch. 42) the author has composed thirty-nine chapters of great Hebrew poetry which demolish the standard view.

At the end of the prologue Job sits in misery among the ashes, and three friends come to see him. These friends will represent the traditional view of evil and thus become foils for Job, but they deserve credit for maintaining another traditional view, that of community—they are there for Job. They naturally assume he has done something to deserve this suffering. When Job proclaims his innocence, they take the logical course and urge him to acknowledge what he has done wrong. How can he be reconciled to God if he denies any wrongdoing? The irony is effective. To admit a wrongdoing would be to lie and thus to do wrong. Job stands his ground, no easy task since he has been brought up with the same viewpoint as his friends.

As the friends persist in trying to get Job to admit how he had sinned, their arguments become more elaborate and increasingly bitter. They ask Job if God can do wrong. They ask if he dares to judge God. All, however, to no avail. Job insists he did no wrong, and he calls on God to acknowledge this. The friends' attitude progressively turns from concern for Job to anger and confusion. As Job steadfastly refuses to admit wrongdoing, he forces his friends to consider the impossible, that maybe they are wrong, maybe there is such a thing as innocent suffering, maybe suffering does not result solely from divine retribution for evil. Eventually Job reduces his thoroughly shaken friends to silence. At this point in the story a young man named Elihu appears (chs. 32–37), advancing the traditional argument by pointing out the redemptive nature of suffering, but he too fails to move Job who insists that only God can answer him.

To Job's surprise, God does.

God speaks to Job out of a whirlwind, demanding that Job answer questions, mostly about the creation and the natural world. "Where were you when I laid the foundation of the earth? . . . when the morning stars sang together and all the heavenly beings shouted for joy?" (38:6–7). God compares his power to Job's: "Can you draw out Leviathan with a fishhook?" (41:1). God even resorts to sarcasm: "Who determined its [the earth's] measurements? Surely you know!" (38:5). The reader finds this uncomfortable. Has not Job suffered enough? Does God really have to treat him this way?

But such treatment is essential to the author's answer to the question of why a good and powerful deity permits evil. For him, God is simply beyond human ability to comprehend. His intimidating speech emphasizes the gap between divine and human; even a good man like Job cannot bridge it. For some horribly inexplicable reason, a deity who could prevent evil and innocent suffering allows them to happen. Humans can never understand why he does what he does; they can only trust that he cares for them and that somehow innocent suffering does not obviate God's providential care for humans. Ultimately Job acknowledges this: "Therefore I uttered what I did not understand, things too wonderful for me, which I did not know" (42:3).

Although the contrived ending pacified traditionalists by suggesting that the old system still worked, this anonymous author had produced a brilliant and revolutionary theodicy. God permits innocent suffering and does not reveal why because we cannot understand his ways.

The author of Job advanced the question of evil by insisting that innocent suffering occurs. He also insisted that he and his fellow Jews had to acknowledge and somehow trust a deity who appears distant and silent at times of great crisis when his people need to feel his presence the most. Many Christians would also agree with this; Job has always been a popular book for theologians. Job's theodicy, incomprehensibility combined with a faith in divine providence, is a difficult one, but, for religious people, it may be the only one.

Among the many Christians attracted to Job's argument was the great modern Catholic theologian, the German Jesuit Karl Rahner (1904–1984). In learned fashion, he dismisses the notion that suffering in this life is necessary for a heavenly afterlife:

> For no one can prove that this suffering is the absolute necessary means for attaining to eternal life. . . . If, moreover, eternal life cannot simply be used as a way of brushing away the history of cruelty, then a crudely understood future state of happiness does not justify the horrors that preceded it.

Rahner does look for the easy way out. People can attain eternal life without suffering, which in turn means that suffering is not necessary for eternal life. We cannot facilely explain evil away by claiming that God will "make it up" to us after death. Rahner insists that we must face the problem head on.

Rahner considered and rejected a variety of explanations for innocent human suffering, such as evil as a product of freedom or as a way to produce morally mature creatures who struggle against it. He concluded that suffering is incomprehensible, but

> This mystery of God's incomprehensibility, however, is not merely the mystery of a being to be understood as static, but is also the mystery of God's freedom, of his underivable disposition, which has not to be justified before any other authority. . . . *The incomprehensibility of suffering is part of the incomprehensibility of God.* . . . Suffering, then, is the form . . . in which the incomprehensibility of God himself appears.

Believers can only approach God in love, a love

> dispossessing man until he is absorbed selflessly into the mystery of God. . . .

Rahner did not hide suffering behind God's incomprehensibility but rather contended that God in his essential being is beyond our comprehension, and God's permitting evil to exist is one manifestation of this reality. Human acceptance of this fact is more than just a way to explain the coexistence of God and evil; it is how we approach God in his totality.

> . . . in our present concrete state, *the acceptance of suffering without an answer other than the incomprehensibility of God and his freedom is the concrete form in which we accept God himself and allow him to be God* (*Theological Investigations* 19, 205–207).

When Rahner speaks of the "acceptance of suffering," he does not mean that we should not try to do our best to alleviate suffering but rather that we must accept the incomprehensibility of God's permitting suffering to occur. God's incomprehensibility challenged the ancient Jews and now it challenges modern Christians. It may be inescapable as a theodicy.

APPENDIX: A Brief Word about Purely Human Approaches to Evil

This is a book for believers by a believer, but we must consider briefly purely human approaches to evil, specifically by the sciences. Many religious people wrongly believe that science and religion have a long history of antagonism, but that derives mostly from two events, the condemnation of Galileo in the seventeenth century and the opposition to Darwin in the nineteenth century. Clearly in both cases religious people, especially those in authority, overreacted because of insufficient understanding of the scientific issues at hand. But we should also remember that many of science's greatest names, such as Copernicus and Newton, were quite religious, and even today many scientists are believers, while the Vatican has a famous astronomical observatory. Furthermore, if science and religion are at odds, why do religiously affiliated high schools, colleges, and universities have science departments?

Problems arise when science and religion cross into one another's territories without understanding the nature of the terrain. We religious people have to deal with evil as a problem for those who believe in God but also as a problem for which God and his Church offer resources. Scientists, even believing scientists, cannot bring God or divine revelation or ecclesiastical teaching into their calculations and experiments. That does not mean that what they are doing is contrary to religion but rather independent of it. Religious people can learn much from scientific investigation into evil. To cite an obvious example, people in many ministries, including spiritual counseling, usually have some background in psychology if not formal degrees in that field.

In the late nineteenth century what we call the social sciences came into being, that is, those sciences which study humans as social beings. The social sciences, particularly sociology and psychology, did not set out to deal specifically with evil, but they did teach us all a lot about it.

Sociology has an immediate relevance for us. It deals with how we act as members of groups, such as ethnic, religious, economic, and the like. But sociology has also demonstrated how social groups affect our values, sometimes sadly, sometimes tragically.

Two high school girls are friends because they share so much in common. They both sing in the school chorus, both are on the volleyball team, both write for the school newspaper. One day one of the girls gets a chance to join the coolest clique in school, but the girls in that clique want only her, not her friend. If she joins the clique, she will be doing things with its other members and not with her friend. She finds herself torn and possibly even recognizes that she faces a moral choice. But she is a high school girl, for whom fitting in means so much, even if she thinks the clique girls are rather shallow and more concerned with their looks and clothing than anything else. The moral choice may be clear to us, yet social factors bear heavily upon a teenager. This is a made-up story, and I would like to give it a happy ending by saying that she will stay with her friend, but I will not give it an ending because no clear ending presents itself. Many parents and certainly those readers in education or counseling will recognize the real—for a high school girl—dilemma that she faces. To be sure, this is a minor tragedy compared to some other things we have mentioned, but it is an everyday one that demonstrates how social forces, not inherently evil or good, impact our understanding of right and wrong. No student, not even in the most religious of schools, can escape such pressures.

No doubt readers who work in ghetto areas would tell me that they would love to have problems like this to deal with. I would not disagree. In many poor areas, young people cannot, for their own safety, afford to be alone. But often the dominant local group is the gang, which routinely engages in brutality and often in criminal activities. Most of us like to think that we would rise above such things, but we do not live in ghettoes and we do not know how important it is for inner-city children, especially boys, to belong. For poor children who are despoiled of their humanity by the relentless materialism which tells them that they are what they possess, gang membership provides an alternative to consumerist culture. In a frightening book, *Monster: The Autobiography of an L.A. Gang Member,* Sanyika Shakur describes how he wanted to join a gang to have the feeling of belonging and of being an important "man" (he was twelve) in "the hood." The "initiation ritual" involved enduring a beating from several gang members for the boy to prove he could "take it," and then he had to join the gang in a crime. As he got older, Shakur graduated to more and more serious criminal activities, finally including murder. He wrote the book from his jail cell in the hopes of alerting society to what was going on and, maybe, just maybe, to deter some other ghetto boy from following his path.

Sociology may not deal directly with evil or religion, but none of us can ignore the impact of social pressures on the moral decisions that we have to make. We are not morally bound by our age, education, or economic status, but they do partly influence, both positively and negatively, how we understand right and wrong.

Psychology has had the most significant impact on our understanding of evil. Whereas previous generations would have labeled a child a "bad" boy or girl, modern counselors want to know what kind of home the child comes from. In recent years the public has become very aware of the appalling phenomenon of spousal and child abuse. As professionals have studied it, one factor stands out beyond all others. Abusers are very likely to have been abused themselves when they were children.

This factor is neither universal nor determinative. Some abusers do not come from that background, and many abused children grow up to be caring adults. Yet the statistics make it clear that an abusive childhood stands behind many incidents of abuse by adults.

These statistics impact the notion of evil because they prove that an abusive childhood has diminished the ability of many people to make a moral judgment, to see abuse as something evil, and to realize that understanding rather than violence is the way to deal with problems. Some people make an immoral judgment to abuse, but others make an amoral judgment; they simply think that violence is an acceptable method of handling marital or family difficulties. Recognizing the psychological background of the abuser does not make child or spousal abuse acceptable or even morally neutral, but it does make it clear that the choice between good and evil acts is almost never an objective one of deciding between two clear alternatives.

This is now largely accepted in society. Media stories routinely point out how the teenage prostitute was seduced by her father or the teenage thief was neglected by his mother. Knowing this background does not cause us to ignore the crimes, but it does explain, at least partially, why they occurred. It will also often mitigate society's view of the offender, who deserves counseling rather than jail. No one today would discuss someone's evil acts without considering the psychological factors involved.

Some religious people fear psychology because they believe it will lead to determinism, that is, the belief that people make no moral choices but simply act in a predetermined way. In this scenario, people have no free will but simply do what their environment conditioned them to do, that is, their background "determined" their behavior. This fear is unfounded. Psychological factors impact what we do but do not determine it; as we just noted, not all abused children grow up to be abusers. If their background determined their future, the percentage of abusers should be 100 percent. Furthermore, as counselors and therapists and school psychologists know, behavior can be changed. People do heal.

The scientific impact on evil still goes on. Now that the Human Genome Project has been completed, people will wonder about how much genetics may influence human behavior. Many of those people dealing with this issue will be Christians in the sciences, in teaching, or in the helping professions.

Religious people know that life has a more than human dimension, and we certainly know that evil cannot be treated as a purely human phenomenon. In "The Lame Shall Enter First," discussed in the previous chapter, Flannery O'Connor gave us an alarming picture of what happens when someone does that. But the awareness of a spiritual dimension should not lead us to disparage or ignore the wonderful, productive work of people who, following professional standards, have often told us much about how social and psychological forces can impact moral decisions and even our understanding of evil. As we have noted, many scientists are believers who do their professional work without bringing in the spiritual but for whom there is a more than scientific dimension to problems. Furthermore, those of us, especially those in counseling or ministry, who want to help people with the spiritual dimension of a problem should never discount its human dimension. These are two aspects of a problem, and they are not in opposition. In fact, more than one Christian psychologist has told me that, after reading the Gospels, they concluded—professionally—that Jesus had real psychological insights into human nature. Not a bad example to follow.

Some Questions for Reflection and Discussion

1. Is it necessary to try to understand how God and evil can coexist or should we just accept that they do?

2. Can you think of other explanations of evil besides the ones described in this chapter?

3. How can we draw the line between harmful relativism and just not wanting to interfere in people's lives?

4. Do modern Christians, deliberately or inadvertently, view Muslims as the Other? If so, what can we do about it? Are the roles reversed in the Middle East? Are Westerners, especially Christians, seen as the Other?

5. If you are glad that you exist, can you think of evil events that made your existence possible? How do you feel, knowing that your existence derives partly from the suffering of others?

6. Are we uncomfortable with the idea of a God who changes in response to his interaction with his creatures? Or does this idea make God seem less distant? Does a loving relationship necessarily change those persons involved, whether human or divine?

7. This chapter referred several times to the Oklahoma City Memorial. Can you name other memorials that are civic or secular but still convey religious or spiritual feelings?

8. What current scientific projects do you think will change our understanding of evil? Why?

3

Responses to Evil

We know what evil does to us, and we know that the existence of evil does not negate the existence of God or of divine providence. Believers are fundamentally optimists. We believe in a good God who will help us to overcome even the most desperate of challenges, so now, with God's help, let us see how we can and must respond to evil.

Let us start by returning very briefly to the earlier chapters. We cannot respond to evil unless we accept its existence, take it seriously, and recognize what it really is.

Evil exists. It is vicious, hurtful, and dangerous. We cannot wish it away with platitudes like "It's all for the best," nor can we resort to relativism to pretend that evil is only something that we create in our minds. These approaches represent unreality at its worst.

We must take evil seriously as a factor in our lives. Hokey 1940s movies about Catholic priests and nuns used to show Sister Superior telling Father Pastor, "Don't worry, Father. God will provide." God *will* provide, but we should still worry. God's *provide*nce does not exonerate us from taking responsibility for our lives and for making our own decisions. When evil challenges us, God will provide help, but we must still do our own part.

Since the first chapter dealt with what evil does to us as individuals and groups, it also showed us how we can recognize it, but here we can recognize one more basic thing about evil. We will take it from that most difficult of biblical books, Revelation. For all its vivid imagery, such as the New Jerusalem, the pearly gates, and streets of gold, Christians have never liked this book very much, and it is not hard to see why. Revelation deals in a visionary way with the final conflict between good and evil, and the victorious God promptly consigns the wicked off to eternal damnation without mercy and without giving them a chance to

repent. To be sure, most Christians understand their faith quite differently, but Revelation does give us one valuable insight into evil that we
should keep constantly in mind as we respond to it. This biblical book
stresses the absolute separation of good and evil. The two have nothing
in common; they have no shared ground; the good cannot compromise
with evil or deal with evil in any other way than as a threat. We will
never respond successfully to evil if we ignore these realities. But to this
salutary teaching we must add an important qualifier: we must always
distinguish the evil act from the person doing it. In the words of St.
Augustine, "Hate the sin, love the sinner."

There are probably as many ways to respond to evil as there are forms
of it. I make no claim to have listed them all, but I would like to take a
twofold approach. First, let us consider how the basic teachings of
Scripture and the Church can aid us. Second, let us learn from victims
of evil about how they dealt with it.

Years ago my university invited the distinguished Anglican theologian Norman Pittenger to give a series of lectures on modern theology.
He dealt partly with why so many people have a negative view of Christianity. He told the audience, "When I want to know why some people
think ill of Christianity, I look in the mirror." He implied, of course, that
all of us in the audience should look in the mirror, too.

When it comes to evil, we should, like the environmentalists, think
globally and act locally. Are we forces for good or evil? Admittedly, few
of us are actual forces for evil in the way that criminals are, but are we
really forces for the good? Are the people we come in contact with better or worse for having interacted with us? Did we really take an interest in them? Did we really listen to what they said, or did we act like the
Pharisee in Luke's parable, parading our goodness for others to appreciate? We can never forget that goodness must start somewhere, and it
can start with us, but does it?

We could multiply points like these, but we must also be on guard so
that *we do not expect too much of ourselves*. We will try to do the good, and
we will fail, and so we will have to try again—we are only human. We
must learn to live with our shortcomings and not to magnify them so
that they depress us. To speak personally, one of the most difficult
things about writing a book on evil is that it constantly reminds me of
my own failures. More and more I find myself asking, "Who are you to
write a book about evil for others? You are not special. You are a sinner,
just like everyone else." And that is precisely the point. All of us, even
the greatest of saints, are sinners, and the great saints recognized that.
We have seen how St. Augustine agonized about his boyish theft of
pears. St. Patrick of Ireland identified himself in his literary works as
Ego, Patricius, peccator, that is, "I, Patrick, the sinner." The sixteenth-

century Spanish mystic, St. Theresa of Avila, constantly wrote about her sinful nature and her wickedness. If sinners did not write books about evil, there would be no books about evil. To apply these insights to myself, I know that this book and its author are inadequate to such a daunting topic, but I cannot let that keep me from writing. We can do no good by obsessing on our shortcomings.

Our evil deeds are functions of our whole persons. For Christians, God and the Church offer many resources, such as Scripture, the sacraments, a community of fellow believers, opportunities for charitable works, great religious literature, and the confidence that although evil will triumph frequently in individual episodes, God will triumph in the end. We know that there are many good, caring people in whose lives God and the Church play no role, and we Christians must be thankful to God that we have such people and we must believe that God works somehow through them. But our concern here is what Christians can do. An active faith life can be a strong antidote to evil. As we draw strength from our Christianity, we strengthen our ability to do good in the world and maybe even to convince others of the value they too can get from these sources that inspire us.

But can we single out some specifics that are available to all of us? Yes, there are the three virtues that the Apostle Paul singled out in 1 Corinthians 13: faith, hope, and love. These virtues can play many roles in the lives of Christians, but let us focus on ways that those virtues may help us to respond to evil.

Faith

Faith has two aspects, personal commitment and intellectual adherence. On the commitment level, faith involves, first and foremost, trust in someone else. Often we have faith in those we know, and we always have faith in those we love. We do not see those persons as flawless, but we know in our hearts that these people want to do good for us. They may let us down, but they do not mean to do so. Conversely, people have faith in us, and we may let them down but we would never do so deliberately. When we have faith, we belong to a community, a community of people linked by affection and trust. When we have religious faith, we are again linked to a community of people, but we are also linked to God and to believers throughout the world as well as those who went before us and those who will come after us—in traditional phrasing, the communion of saints.

Viewing faith in this way enables us to deal with evil on several fronts. We realize that we do not have to face evil alone. To use an everyday analogy, think of how people join groups or clubs to help them lose weight or to exercise more. They know the value of group involvement and encouragement. So it is with the challenge of evil. We can draw strength from the community by just knowing that there are others who face the challenges we do. More than that, in a faith community, we can see evidence of goodness triumphing over evil.

As I am writing this, my local suburban parish is working with homeless people from inner-city Cleveland, providing them with meals and clothing and helping them to find housing. Every year our parish helps to feed people in poorer parishes and also those in our own parish. We do this personally, not just by writing checks. We also send parish teams to Honduras to help in building homes for the poor. Yes, we could always do more, but these charitable works show us the impact of goodness. We can see people of faith making a difference for those who suffer from evil. We personally experience the value of a faith community.

All members of a faith community suffer, but we know that there are those who suffer more. Working to help others brings to mind the evils they suffer and our common effort to alleviate those evils. In doing so we recognize that our own suffering is not so unusual and that a community would be there for us.

But sometimes people in need are too self-conscious or embarrassed to turn to a community for help. When I was a boy, my father ran a local volunteer food program. Sometimes the recipients would come to our home to pick up the food, and my father told my brothers and me to go to our rooms and wait there until he told us we could come out. That was because some of the recipients were the parents of our schoolmates, and they were embarrassed that we would know that they were in need. My father also realized that small children could not keep secrets, so he was right to send us to our rooms. My father was a good man who could never consciously hurt anyone, and although people did not use phrases like "faith community" in the 1950s, he knew how to care sensitively for those in that community.

Even if we do not feel comfortable dealing privately with our local community, we still have a community with God—indeed, the Trinity itself is the archetype of a loving community. We also have those Christians who went before us.

My personal favorites are Thomas More and Dorothy Day. More was a husband and a father, a successful writer, a wealthy noble, and a powerful man who served as chancellor of England under King Henry VIII. He enjoyed the goods that this life can offer, and he did not want to lose them. Yet in the crunch, he risked and lost all that he had, even his life, rather than compromise his conscience. Dorothy Day, whose autobiography makes fine spiritual reading, devoted her life to helping the poor and opposing war, both when she was a socialist and after she became a Catholic. She triumphed over a personal life that went against most Christian values. If, as many American Catholics hope, Dorothy Day is someday canonized, she will be the first woman Catholic saint who had live-in lovers as well as an abortion.

I certainly make no claim to be a Dorothy Day or Thomas More; just the reverse, their struggles for sanctity make mine look puny. But I draw inspiration from their lives and from the knowledge that they and I belong, however distant, to the same community of believers.

In recent decades, the intellectual element of faith has been downplayed, a consequence of the excessive stress put upon it earlier when faith was routinely defined in theology textbooks as giving intellectual adherence to propositions. If you believed in the Incarnation, you had faith. True, but the shallowness of such an approach was criticized as early as the first century and in the Bible itself. Worrying about those who thought that belief without doing good to others was sufficient for salvation, the Epistle of James caustically pointed out, "Even the demons believe in [God]" (2:19).

On the other hand, we do not want to play down the intellectual element too much. The American writer Mark Twain, a morbid atheist late in his life, contemptuously defined faith as believing what you knew was not true. In a word, believers are stupid. We reject Twain's acid cynicism, but we must simultaneously make sure that we do not have "blind" faith, that is, a mindless acceptance of traditional views and attitudes. As we saw in the previous chapter, the coexistence of evil with a good God presents a formidable intellectual problem for Christians, and evil is hardly the one issue that does. Faith is a gift from God that enables us to intellectually apprehend what we could not reach by reason alone, such as the Trinity and the Incarnation. If we believe what we cannot prove by reason alone, we must do so intelligently. We cannot believe in a frivolous or light-hearted way that God will overcome evil. We must know what it is and what problems it poses for the believer.

We can strengthen our personal faith as well as that of our community by taking intellectual questions seriously, by reading the Scriptures, by joining or forming a parish book discussion group (eight other people and my wife and I have been in one for sixteen years), or by attending adult education classes or lectures on theological topics at local seminaries or religiously-affiliated colleges and universities. Ignorance is no friend of faith.

Hope

"Hope springs eternal in the human breast" wrote the English Catholic poet Alexander Pope (1688–1744), and he was almost right. Hope enables us to see beyond even the worst situations, to believe that somehow things can get better—maybe not right away, maybe not in the immediate future, maybe never back to what they had been before some sad event occurred, but better than they are now and possibly better than they had been before but in a new and different way. We know that God could bring good out of evil, an experience we have all had and to which I alluded to earlier when talking about Oklahoma City and September 11.

But, contrary to Alexander Pope, hope does not spring eternally in every human breast. Some people suffer from the evil of despair. The English word "despair" comes from a Latin verb meaning "to be without hope." While comparatively few people despair, this will give us an opportunity to see hope at its most effective against evil.

People who despair believe that their lives cannot ever become better, and that no one, not their family members nor friends nor even God, can do anything to help—if they even care. Sometimes despair leads to emotional or psychological breakdowns, and sometimes it leads to suicide. I knew a young man who committed suicide. I have always wondered how he arrived at such a bleak view of his life that he lost any desire to live. True despair represents the impact of evil at its worst.

Into the twentieth century religious people did not understand this phenomenon very well. It was common for churches to refuse Christian burial to people who took their own lives. They justified this on the grounds that suicide was a mortal sin, and since the person who committed that sin was dead at the completion of the act, she or he could not repent and thus went to hell. Now, thank God, we have moved away from that terrible, juridical approach. We try to understand despair, its causes, and its potential cure.

As people of hope, Christians have trouble understanding those who despair. We cannot grasp why a family member or friend has become so burdened with life's setbacks so as to think that she or he has no future. We also cannot understand why this person cannot turn to God. We naturally see our task as trying to convince that person to hope, but we must realize that we cannot do it with a "pep talk." We must remember that despair is not a sin but a human condition that did not occur overnight, that our relative or friend arrived at this state of affairs after a period of disappointment, maybe one that had been years in developing, such as a failed marriage or estrangement from the family or the daily depression of a dead-end job.

To share with this person the hope that we have as Christians, we must take his or her problems seriously, even if we think that we could have handled them without falling into despair. We must acknowledge the depth of these problems, and we must listen pastorally while the person talks them out. Indeed, just being there and listening may give the person some hope by proving that someone cares. Evil has been around for a long time, and it has worked daily to bring this person to such a sorry state. Just because hope, if given a chance by a despairing person, will always triumph does not mean that the triumph will be easy or quick.

We have looked at hope in terms of our helping other people. We too are not immune from the threat of despair, and when we turn faithfully to hope, we should remember this: Despair means that evil has won. Nothing combats Evil so directly as hope. Hope tells Evil, "You have not won. We will not give up on ourselves or others because God never gives up on us."

Love—the Ultimate Antidote to Evil

When the Apostle Paul called love the greatest of these three virtues (1 Cor 13:3), he did so because of its permanence. When we are one with God forever, we will not need faith because we will know him, nor will we need hope because all our hopes will have been fulfilled, yet we will still love God and the entire communion of saints.

In a well-known (because it is often read at weddings) passage (1 Cor 13:4-13), Paul discoursed on the nature of love. "Love is patient; love is kind; love is not envious or boastful or arrogant . . . . it does not rejoice in wrongdoing, but rejoices in the truth." His list goes on, but we can see that, fundamentally, love reaches out and focuses itself upon others. All the examples we saw of evil show people who put themselves first— Adam and Eve, Victor Frankenstein, Sheppard, and all of Dante's self-absorbed sinners. Evil pushes us to put ourselves first, ahead of everyone, even God, and ahead of everything, even the common good or the welfare of the planet we live on.

Love does not push us but rather enables us to be personally fulfilled by doing for others, paralleling, however inadequately, what God does for others and with no limits. "For God so loved the world that he sent his only-begotten Son to save it."

St. Augustine once wrote, "Love God and do as you please." His reasoning is sound. If we love God, we can do as we please because then we can only do good. Moving this saying from the divine to the human, we cannot harm anyone we truly love. Love is demanding, and developing a loving relationship takes time and effort. With all respect to Augustine, it is usually easier to love God than to love many of his creations. When we hear the famous saying of the humorist Will Rogers, "I never met a man I didn't like," we always think of someone we would like to introduce to him.

But we must give love a chance. We cannot love everyone the way we love those closest to us, but since we can love God, we can love the image and likeness of God in all people. That does not mean that we overlook their faults but rather that we try to look past those faults to the potentially good person inside, just as we hope that people will look past our faults. Think of the times that you have had a bad day and may have been irritable or impatient or distracted. Would you want to be judged by the day when you were at your worst?

In the most important guide to Christian living, the Sermon on the Mount, Jesus said, "Do not judge, so that you may not be judged." He went on, "Why do you see the speck in your neighbor's eye, but do not notice the log in your own eye?" (Matt 7:1-3). Love does not judge but instead seeks for the best. Let us love as best we can—haltingly, with difficulty, perhaps with some failures, but eventually with success. As long as we are able to love, we keep evil at bay.

Let us close this brief look at love and evil by returning to Dante's *Inferno*. You may recall that contrary to medieval tradition of Satan's being consumed by never-ending flames, Dante encased him in ice. Evil brings death, which Dante brilliantly symbolized with eternal cold. The link between death and evil goes back to the Garden of Eden when Adam and Eve's disobedience brought death to the world. The image of personified evil's being encased in ice makes the lifelessness of death more striking. Love we associate with warmth, sometimes the physical warmth of a hug, sometimes the emotional warmth of being around those we care for. When we love, the warmth of love melts the cold of evil. God is love personified, and in Dante's epic he is as physically far from evil as it is possible to be, a symbol of the unbridgeable gap between love and evil. One simply cannot exist in the presence of the other, and that is why we call love the ultimate antidote to evil.

Faith, hope, and love are virtues God gives to us all; they are ours to accept or reject. We can use them to forestall the evils that oppress us all. But some evils oppress specific groups in particular ways, so we will now turn to two very distinctive ways of dealing with evil, ways that have evolved among those who are oppressed by violence and hatred. These ways do not work independently of faith, hope, and love, but they do stress other approaches to dealing with evil. The first way is that of forgiveness and reconciliation; the second is that of redemptive suffering.

Forgiveness and Reconciliation

Evil divides us. In Genesis evil separated the human race from God and from nature, and it separated humans from one another as Adam tried to pass the responsibility for his disobedience to Eve (3:12). Evil divides families, friends, and nations. Christianity teaches us that we can overcome this divide by forgiveness and reconciliation. We turn once again to the Gospel of Luke.

Luke, and only he, records the Parable of the Prodigal Son (15:11-32), which Scripture scholars believe would be better called the Parable of the Two Brothers. The story is well known. An arrogant young man decides that he does not want to wait for his father to die to get his inheritance, and so he asks his father for the funds immediately. In spite of his son's unspeakable rudeness, the father acquiesces and gives him his inheritance, which the young man squanders "in dissolute living." Destitute, he takes a lowly job feeding pigs. Since the Jews were forbidden even to touch pigs, we can imagine the revulsion this image caused among the Jews who heard Jesus tell this parable.

This degradation brings the young man to his senses. He decides to return home and beg his father's forgiveness. When he arrives home and apologizes, his father welcomes him warmly and even orders the servants to kill "the fatted calf" for a feast of rejoicing. All in all, this is a moving story of youthful dereliction, parental forgiveness, and familial reconciliation. Except for one detail.

The father has a second son, an older one, who stood by his father, who worked the fields, and who proved himself respectful and reliable. Luke suggests that the father took this son for granted because the son rebukes his father for not giving him "even a young goat so that I might celebrate with my friends," and yet this disreputable younger brother is treated as if he had done nothing wrong. Naturally most of us identify with this older brother. We cannot conceive of saying to our parents, "I don't feel like waiting until you die. Give me the money now." And, like the older brother, we often feel that the good we do goes unappreciated.

But the evangelist has used this character with whom we can identify to set a trap for his readers. Using our identification with the older brother, Luke challenges us:

> *The older brother should be disappointed with his father, right? Right!*
> *The older brother should be furious with his younger brother, right? Right!*
> *The older brother should not forgive his younger brother, right? Uh, well . . .*
> *um . . . not exactly . . . you know . . . I mean, he shouldn't . . . you know*
> *. . . I guess he sort of really should, like, kind of forgive him.*

Exactly, and we can see how Luke has succeeded brilliantly by involving his readers with this parable.

The older brother's resentment may be understandable, but resentment cannot become the standard for his dealings with his family. Luke teaches us that even if forgiveness may be difficult, we must still practice it. Can the older brother let himself be divided from his father and brother when forgiveness would reconcile them? Does he truly want a life of bitter separation instead of reconciling love? As Luke shows us, as a basically good person, the older brother really has no choice but to do the right thing.

Another great literary artist, the French author Victor Hugo (1802–1885), showed the need for reconciliation in a very different and vivid way. In his novel *Les Misérables*, the escaped convict Jean Valjean is pursued by the merciless detective Javert. The detective learns that in the years since his escape, Valjean has become a good man, helping others and even becoming mayor of a town (under a pseudonym). On one occasion, when the police captured a man they thought to be Valjean, thus guaranteeing that the search for him would be called off, the real Valjean identified himself so that the innocent man would not go to prison. But none of this remarkable goodness reaches Javert's cold heart, and when Valjean escapes again, Javert pursues him relentlessly.

Toward the end of the novel, Javert falls into Valjean's power, and he assumes that the convict will kill him to be finally free. But Valjean's goodness rises to the challenge. Not only does he not kill the detective, he actually forgives Javert and releases him. He cannot exact revenge upon him, not even for decades of persecution. Yet events take a frightening twist. Merciless retribution has become Javert's whole life, and it has rendered him incapable of dealing with forgiveness. He cannot understand Valjean, whose mercy has called the detective's values into question. Crushed that he owes his life to Valjean, Javert can find no reason to live. He despairs. He commits suicide. A man of hate driven to suicide because he could not endure another man's goodness—what a remarkable plot. And what a striking image of how evil divides us. Valjean offers Javert a chance to leave hate behind, but he cannot take it.

We can see the value of forgiveness and reconciliation to overcome the divisiveness of evil, but are there not some evils so horrible that, try as we might, we find forgiveness and reconciliation beyond our reach?

The American Mennonite Howard Zehr has worked for years with crime victims who suffered from acts committed against them or against those they loved. His work convinced him that the legal system does little for victims, but also that "unless churches take up their vital parts, change will be slow in coming" ("Restoring Justice," p. 131).

Western societies have responded to crimes with the three Rs: revenge, retribution, and restoration. Revenge is a sin, and one that causes an endless round of counter revenge, as the modern history of the Balkans has proved.

Retribution is the response that dominates our legal systems. "If you do the crime, you do the time." Retribution offers the consolation of a score's having been evened, but it does not attempt to change the character of the offender, who is simply locked up, nor does it do anything for the needs of victims. Modern justice systems see crime as an offense against the state, not the individual, and if the state is satisfied with retribution, the matter is settled. This system reflects the dated attitudes of the Christians who created it, people who saw sin solely as an offense against God who would inflict punishment upon the sinner. But crimes and sins are committed against other people, dividing them from one another, and both victims and offenders need more than just retribution.

Zehr writes, "*The justice of restoration* is essentially harm-focused, meaning that the victims' rights and needs are essential, not peripheral . . . offenders are encouraged to understand the harm they have caused and to take responsibility for it" (p. 132). This sounds strange at first, but restorative justice (which is Zehr's term for justice that reconciles people) characterizes the approaches of many peoples, including Native Americans and the Maori of New Zealand.

Restorative justice does not mean that criminals go free to commit more crimes, but that they become aware of the impact of their crimes on real people. A purse snatching may be a minor event in the eyes of a thief, but the victim may have a lifelong fear of going out alone. The offender may not care that he has violated an impersonal legal system, but he may care that he has hurt someone.

Zehr also stresses the needs of victims. "For Christians . . . pain represents a failure . . . a failure of God's presumed control over the world" (p. 138). Victims think that the order of the world, God's providence, is absent. They feel that a crime has robbed them of their autonomy (such as feeling safe when going out alone) and has consequently dehumanized them. They also feel that their victimhood has cut them off from others, even from other Christians, who do not want to hear their discomforting story. Zehr quotes a woman who survived sexual abuse:

> I feel very trapped and afraid that I won't make it sometimes. Is there hope for people like me? The Church hasn't been much help to me. I have felt that I am an outcast with a deadly disease, and people want to stay away from me. They don't want to hear how I was doing; they just said that God would take care of it. But I am often angry with God and still have a problem relating to God. But nobody wants to hear that either (p. 150).

Evil has divided her from her fellow Christians, who find her situation so delicate that they prefer to keep her at a distance rather than reintegrate her into the community.

Those working in restorative justice are optimists. As Christians, they believe that all people—both offenders and victims—can be made whole, but they can only do so in a community. Criminals often find themselves excluded from the larger community because of poverty or social injustice, and they use crimes to win respect among their peers by showing their *power over others*, which only separates them from others even more. Victims often feel that their suffering has differentiated them from others in the group and that no one wants to hear about their suffering, even though they need more than ever to connect with others. Bringing people together, including sometimes offender and victim, enables people to form or restore communities, thus making forgiveness and reconciliation possible and overcoming the evil of divisiveness.

But even to achieve reconciliation, how can a victim just overlook what happened? *The victim should not overlook the evil,* says Dan Allender, a Christian therapist. He observes, "Forgiveness is too often seen as merely an exercise in releasing bad feelings and ignoring past harm, pretending all is well. Yet nothing could be further from the truth" ("'Forgive and Forget' and Other Myths of Forgiveness," p. 201). We cannot forget a hurt, and we should not try. We should also recognize that resentment of the offender and the desire for vengeance are typical. Forgiveness is not about erasing normal feelings. Allender defines forgiveness: "To forgive another means to cancel a debt in order to open a door for opportunity for both repentance and restoration of the broken relationship" (p. 209). This applies not only to victims of serious offenses but to all of us. We want to forgive someone, but we simply cannot forget how his rudeness spoiled what should have been a happy, celebratory day, and so we have failed in obligation to forgive. No, we have not failed, says Allender. *Even the best Christians are only human. Remembering the offense and still being able to forgive is the sign of the true Christian.*

The stunning power of forgiveness and reconciliation to overcome evil can even be effective on the national level. In 1994 the white apartheid government of South Africa ceased to be, and all South Africans, white, black, and "colored," an offensive designation used for Asians and people of diverse backgrounds, voted for a new government. As the incoming president, Nelson Mandela had to decide what to do with the government and police officials of the apartheid regime who had brutalized, tyrannized, and murdered black citizens. The outgoing apartheid government said it wanted amnesty for its members, suggesting that if it were not granted, there could be serious violence. Mandela feared violence—South Africa had endured enough of that—but he also feared that a blanket amnesty would let criminals believe that they had really done nothing wrong, and it would also cause intense resentment among the surviving sufferers and the relatives of the thousands whom the government had put to death. He faced a serious dilemma.

The solution to the dilemma was the Truth and Reconciliation Commission (TRC), founded and headed by that marvelous Christian, Archbishop Desmond Tutu, who had been awarded the Nobel Peace Prize in 1984 for his efforts to bring peace to his country. Tutu approached his task by combining Christian and African notions. Since he was an archbishop, people knew that Christian values would play a role in the TRC's deliberations, but he made clear that these religious values meshed well with traditional African ones: "Retributive justice is largely Western. The African understanding is far more restorative—not so much to punish as to redress or restore a balance that has been knocked askew. The justice we hope for is restorative" (quoted in *Between Vengeance and Forgiveness* by Martha Minow, p. 81).

Emphasizing the truth in TRC, the commission would recommend amnesty only for police and government officials who requested it, that is, they had to acknowledge that they had violated people's rights and worse. They also had to tell the truth about what they had done, that is, they had to face up to themselves as criminals not just in a general way but in all the specifics. Many officials did so, and many found it liberating. After all, some of them had not been able to tell even their families about their "jobs," and many wives and children were shocked at learning what their husbands and fathers had done. This process removed dishonesty not only from the public area but also from the family circle. The commission's openness to the offenders also obviated any chance of serious violence.

But this commission's approach benefited the victims even more than the offenders. The victims had been brutalized, devalued, and marginalized, and they were often meant to feel, as so many victims do, that they bore some responsibility for their situation. For example, one mother lost a child when he was killed by a stray police bullet while he was crossing the street to watch television at a friend's house. She had never forgiven herself for letting him cross that street, until the TRC convinced her "that her private and personal loss was caused by a sociopolitical situation . . . that the police, and not she, had killed her son" (Minow, p. 70).

Like the victims whom Zehr and Allender wrote about, the South African victims needed to tell their stories, they needed people to listen, they needed to be believed, they needed to be affirmed and validated, and they needed to be reintegrated into the community. As you can imagine, many of the stories tore at the hearts of the TRC members and others who attended the proceedings. Victims told of daily beatings and of being kept incommunicado in filthy cells. Some victims did not say much—their maimed bodies and blinded eyes said more. On occasion Archbishop Tutu simply halted the proceedings while he hung his head in grief.

A majority of those who appeared before the commission were women, the real Johannahs of Kathleen O'Connor's retelling of Job. While many of them had themselves been victims of police viciousness, far more told of husbands and sons who were killed or who were locked up and mysteriously committed suicide in their jail cells or who simply disappeared while the apartheid police rigidly stonewalled all attempts by the women to get information about their loved ones. The police stooped to abusing maternal love, threatening to kill children if the mothers did not cooperate with their investigations. Amazing as it sounds, even more horrific stories could have come to light, but the commission compassionately decided not to ask children victims what had happened to them.

I hope these passages were not too disturbing, but I wanted to show how the power of forgiveness and reconciliation can overcome even the most horrible of evils because for all the pain and suffering that was relived at the TRC hearings, the commission's work succeeded. The victims did not have to forgive and forget; on the contrary, they were encouraged to remember and bring their stories to the light. Sympathetic Christians listened to them, and victims whose pain and whose personhood had been ignored by the apartheid regime found themselves being treated as whole persons of inestimable value. Reconciliation was often achieved. Let me quote these extraordinarily Christian words from a South African mother whose son was arrested, tortured, and finally murdered by the police:

> This thing called reconciliation . . . if I am understanding it correctly . . . if it means that this perpetrator, this man who has killed (my son), if it means that he becomes human again, this man, so that I, so that all of us, get our humanity back . . . then I agree, then I support it all (Minow, p. 82).

We can only stand in awe at the depth of her faith, and we can only wonder how many of us in her situation could have uttered those words. We can only hope that we could.

As these noble South Africans have taught us, to the list of those Christian virtues, faith, hope, and love, that can frustrate the designs of evil, we can add forgiveness and reconciliation.

[A footnote to this section: We have spoken of being reconciled to God and to others, but there is also one more person whom we must be able to forgive and be reconciled with. Inevitably, we are most disappointed in ourselves and cannot forget the evils we have done and the hurt that they caused others. But we must be reconciled to *all* God's children. We must learn to forgive and to be reconciled to ourselves, and that is sometimes more difficult than forgiving and being reconciled to others, but it is no less necessary or important.]

Redemptive Suffering

We saw that the great modern Catholic theologian Karl Rahner, S.J., insisted that suffering is not essential to salvation, and it is theoretically possible to live a good Christian life without suffering. But, realistically, all of us do suffer, and we have to wonder if this suffering, if not necessary for salvation, has any purpose. In fact, we have all learned that suffering can bring new insights and new visions. Some years ago I was in a serious accident, and although I was permanently injured, the physical damage was remarkably minor, and I have been able to lead a 99 percent normal life. After the accident, as my family—especially my wife—and my friends provided sympathy and support, I realized in a very powerful way the importance of people and the inane sinfulness of letting minor things come between others and me. Since the accident, I have tried not to let the petty annoyances and foibles of everyday life determine how I view those around me, and I hope that I am convincing them to see me the same way. My guess is that many readers could match this story.

But the notion of redemptive suffering as an antidote to evil requires more than just personal experiences to validate it. It requires some serious theological thinking, although it does *not* require considering every tragedy to be something deliberately sent by God to test us or strengthen us. *God does not intentionally harm us.* People who think like that unknowingly and inadvertently link themselves with those critics of Christianity who have often mocked the notion of the Atonement, the idea that the Son of God had to suffer and die to make us one (at-one-ment) with God. After all, what kind of Father demands the death of his son?

The Scriptures teach us that to redeem humanity, the Son of God *had to become completely human*, save for sin, even to the point of experiencing suffering. The Epistle to the Hebrews tells us that Jesus "in every respect has been tested as we are, yet is without sin" (4:15). "Therefore (Jesus) had to become like his brothers and sisters (that is, all humanity) in every respect so that he might . . . make a sacrifice of atonement for the sins of the people. Because he himself was tested by what he suffered, he is able to help those who are being tested" (2:17-18). Would God have preferred that his Son not suffer? Of course, but when God's Son took on human nature, he had to take on the suffering that goes with it. Rahner was right; God does not *require* that we suffer. But through evil, we humans have made suffering our lot, and *because of us*, the human, incarnate Christ also *had* to suffer. Free of evil himself, he still had to endure the consequences of evil.

So the Bible teaches us that suffering can be redemptive, but is this just one of those biblical ideas that belong to the ancient world and do not have relevance today? No, and to prove its continuing relevance, let us turn to one of the great Christians of our age, the Reverend Doctor Martin Luther King, Jr. (another Nobel Peace Prize recipient, 1964), and to an important, modern woman theologian, Marilyn McCord Adams.

Martin Luther King, Jr.'s life (1929–1968) paralleled that of the apostle Paul. For his beliefs and work, King suffered multiple jailings, beatings, and an attempted murder by stabbing; his home was bombed twice; and he died a violent death. Like the apostle, King realized early on that suffering from evils had become inevitable in his life. While he knew that he could meet head-on the evils facing him, he feared that he might fall into spiritual pride, the third temptation in Luke's Gospel. He wrote, "A person who constantly calls attention to his trials and sufferings is in danger of developing a martyr complex. . . . It is possible for one to be self-centered in his self-denial and self-righteous in his sacrifices" (*Moral Evil and Redemptive Suffering* by Anthony Pinn, p. 225). Bearing this in mind, he spoke of his trials because they strongly formed his view of redemptive suffering.

Having been "battered by the storms of persecution," King was sorely "tempted to retreat to a more quiet and serene life," somewhat reminiscent of Thomas More's reluctance to sacrifice all that he had. "But every time such temptation appeared, something came to strengthen and sustain my determination. I have learned now that the Master's burden is light precisely when we take his yoke upon us" (p. 225).

Accepting his burden, King soon realized that ". . . there were two ways that I could respond to my situation: either to react with bitterness or seek to transform the suffering into a creative force. . . . I have attempted to see my personal ordeals as an opportunity to transform myself and heal the people involved in the tragic situation (of racism and discrimination)" (pp. 225–26). He succeeded in transforming not only himself but also the United States of America; he healed not only African-Americans but all people in this country.

King concluded these thoughts by observing theologically that

> There are some who still find the cross a stumbling block, and others consider it foolishness (1 Cor 1:18), but I am more convinced than ever before that it (the cross of Jesus) is the power of God unto social and individual salvation. So like the Apostle Paul I can now humbly but proudly says, "I bear in my body the marks of the Lord Jesus." The suffering and agonizing moment through which I have passed over the last few years have also drawn me closer to God (p. 226).

There is nothing to add to such insight and eloquence.

Although the best known African-American theologian and pastor to write about moral evil and redemptive suffering, Martin Luther King,

Jr., was just one of many. Howard Thurman (1900–1981) wrote, ". . . that there is a fellowship of suffering as well as community of sufferers." While it is true that "suffering tends to isolate the individual" (p. 237), the recognition that we belong to the community strengthens us to deal with the cause of that suffering.

James Cone (1938–) wrote of the evil of slavery and of how Jesus "was the one who lived with (the slaves) and thereby gave them the courage and strength" to endure until their situation changed. "When everything else in their experience said they were nobodies, Jesus entered their experience as a friend and helper of the weak and helpless" (p. 294).

According to Anthony Pinn, J. Deotis Roberts (1927–) contends that "Christians can make creative use of suffering without understanding suffering as a manifestation of the divine will" (p. 303). God does not will suffering but permits it, and, for Roberts, our creative challenge is to bring redemptive value to our suffering.

The list of writers could go on, and, of course, African-American pastors and theologians are not the only ones who have dealt with this topic. But their experience as a people, the experience of slavery, of Jim Crow, of blatant racism, and of subtle discrimination has crushed many black people and their communities in a way that others cannot comprehend. These writers witness not just to the need of redemptive suffering to deal with such evils but also to its effectiveness. All Christians surely can apply this striking lesson to their own lives.

When the contemporary American theologian Marilyn McCord Adams wrote her essay "Redemptive Suffering: A Christian Solution to the Problem of Evil" (in *The Problem of Evil*, edited by Michael Peterson, pp. 169–87), she opened with the apostle Paul's verse about the apparent foolishness of the cross, the same verse cited by Martin Luther King, Jr. Instead of drawing from personal or group experiences, Adams takes a directly theological approach, asking "How can the suffering of the innocent and loyal at the hands of the guilty and hard-hearted solve the problem of evil? . . . To see . . . how from this starting-point it is possible to arrive at a Christian approach to the problem of evil through redemptive suffering, it is necessary to review briefly the doctrinal presuppositions of such a conclusion" (pp. 169, 173).

Her theology is involved, but the central points are that God made human beings to enter into "non-manipulative relationships of self-surrendering love with himself and relationships of self-giving with others" (p. 173), but he had to give us free will, even though he knew we would misuse it. Here is a major innovation: when we sin, God will judge us, *but* "God's interest in judgment is not condemnation and punishment but forgiveness and reconciliation" (p. 175). Furthermore, as a believing Christian, Adams uses a resource not commonly employed by

theologians, namely, Christian mysticism. She says that when we have
achieved the beatific vision, we will see retrospectively our moments of
suffering as the sources of some good. More than that, we will see them
as "times of sure identification with and vision into the inner life of the
creator" (p. 187).

She wrote this essay in 1986 and returned to the topic in 1999 with
her book *Horrendous Evils and the Goodness of God*. There she insists that
". . . at a minimum, God's goodness to human individuals would require that God guarantee each a life that was a great good to him/her on
the whole by balancing serious evils" (p. 31), the balance not to be
understood in a "bookkeeping" sense, but that "for an individual's life
to be a great good to him/her on the whole, it is not good enough for
good to balance off or defeat evil objectively speaking. The individual
must him/herself also recognize and appropriate at least some . . . positive meanings" (p. 82).

But if we abandon that notion that the relation of individuals' goodness to the evils they have suffered should be seen in a bookkeeping
sense, we should also abandon another traditional idea, the notion of
God's providence as an undeserved gift. The traditional view sees God
as a stern judge who may or may not overlook our faults and who, for
some unknown reason, gives some of us the gift of grace, even though
we do not deserve it. In place of this Adams invokes "the mother-infant
analogy to make room for particular (that is, individual) divine providence. . . ." (p. 104) The old image makes God look so cold. The image
of God as mother far better portrays the image of universal love, which,
ultimately, is what God is. Mothers judge children but with love, and it
does not occur to a mother that her gifts to her children are undeserved.
Why would she not want to give gifts to her children?

And if some spiritual dinosaurs belch out that envisioning God as
mother is just politically correct nonsense, let us recall that the medieval
Catholic mystic Julian of Norwich (1342–1416) and some other mystics
imaged Jesus, a man, as Mother. And if people want to deny validity to
Julian's insight, then let us go right back to the Scriptures themselves. In
Matthew's Gospel, Jesus laments over the city of Jerusalem, "Jerusalem,
Jerusalem, the city that kills the prophets and stones those who are sent
to it! How often have I desired to gather your children together as a hen
gathers *her* brood under *her* wings, and you were not willing!"(Matt
23:37). The Lord himself used a maternal image, and when we recall the
status of women in the ancient world, we can see that this female imagery also identifies Jesus with those who are oppressed.

After Jesus on the cross, what is a better image of redemptive suffering than that of a mother?

We all hope that we and those we love will not suffer, but when evils afflict us, we can, like the Lord, try to bring some redemptive good from those afflictions.

One Question for Reflection and Discussion

Unlike the first two chapters, this one has only one question, but it may end up with many parts:

Name some current evils that are impacting you personally or your local group/community or the larger world, and then decide how you alone or you and others together can respond to these evils.

Some Final Thoughts

It may not be difficult to recognize evil, but it is surely difficult to deal with it. No matter how often we check it, it comes back again. In his novel *Perelandra*, the British author and spiritual writer C. S. Lewis (1898–1963) tells the story of Eve and Adam on Mars or Perelandra as it is called by its inhabitants. This time God sends help in the form of a good man named Ransom who is willing to ransom his life to save the planet. He has to combat an evil being, and he realizes to his horror that his opponent never sleeps, a wonderful symbol of evil's relentlessness. The evil being tells lies, twists Ransom's words around, and turns upside down all the good things Ransom tries to do. This is science fiction, but it tells a real story about the challenges we face.

In the last chapter I cited the environmentalist credo, think globally and act locally. If we cannot make the world a better place, we can make our world a better place for those with whom we interact. We can do little things that make a difference—volunteer for a worthwhile cause, give to charity, or visit someone who is hospitalized. On the personal level, I try to be a good husband, father, teacher, neighbor, and member of my local parish community, and my family and friends are people who are trying to do likewise.

We should also never underestimate our ability to change the larger world. Business people and political figures listen to what people say. To use a business example, a woman in my town wrote to a local supermarket executive to ask why his stores wasted so much paper in wrapping their products. The executive wrote back to say that she was right and that the supermarket was changing its practices. Obviously there is no way to know if it was just her letter or if hers was one of many, but her letter made some difference. As for politics, in the aftermath of September 11, my wife and I joined millions of other Americans in letting our elected representatives know that when the United States attacked Afghanistan, every effort should be made not to harm the millions of

Afghan civilians who did not support terrorists. All these efforts—business, politics, personal—meet with mixed success, but that will not stop me from trying again.

I do not really feel qualified to give lengthy advice to readers about how to respond to evil. We saw in the last chapter what some genuinely heroic Christians have done, and you can certainly learn more from their lives than from any book. And, in the last analysis, we are all good people, made in the divine image and likeness, and we know what we have to do. May God give us the grace to do it.

Let me close with a personal anecdote about a little victory of good over evil, told with the hope that I am not falling into spiritual pride.

Recently I met a former student named Bette. She is a good person, but she has trouble staying focused when she talks. When she starts to talk, she usually goes off on a tangent and never seems to stop. Anyone talking to her waits for the first break in the conversation and then quickly makes up an excuse to leave, something that Bette, who is not stupid, certainly notices.

When I met Bette, I asked her how she was doing. She said a little bit about herself and then started talking about the achievements of her brother, whom she obviously loves and is very proud of, and then about her family's upcoming celebration of Christmas, assuming that all this would interest me. After a few minutes she paused, and I started to make my excuses. I saw by the expression on her face that this is what she expected me to do. Then it suddenly hit me that this is how everyone treats her. I, who was writing a book about evil, was about to do the same hurtful thing.

I was immensely disappointed with myself yet simultaneously desirous of doing the right thing, so I asked Bette if there was anything else going on in her life. She first looked surprised and then very pleased. "Oh, yes, Dr. Kelly, just last week I. . . ." Five minutes later *she* told *me* that she had to leave. I told her how much I had enjoyed talking with her and that I hoped we would meet again soon, and she said she hoped so, too.

I felt wonderful because I had probably done more good in those ten minutes than I would do for the rest of the week. And, a bit to my surprise but much to my delight, I realized that I truly did hope that Bette and I would meet again soon.

Further Reading

Adams, Marilyn McCord. *Horrendous Evils and the Goodness of God.* Ithaca, New York: Cornell University Press, 1999.

_____. "Redemptive Suffering: A Christian Solution to the Problem of Evil" in *The Problem of Evil*, edited by Michael Peterson, 169–87.

Allender, Dan. "'Forgive and Forget' and Other Myths of Forgiveness," in *God and the Victim: Theological Reflections on Evil, Victimization, Justice, and Forgiveness*, edited by Lisa Barnes and Michael Shattuck, Grand Rapids, Mich.: William B. Eerdmans, 2000, 199–216.

Dante. *The Inferno.* Translated by Mark Musa. New York: Penguin Books, 1984.

Fagan, Sean. "Original Sin," in *The Modern Catholic Encyclopedia*, edited by Michael Glazier and Monika Hellwig, Collegeville: The Liturgical Press, 1994, 620–22.

Hasker, William. "On Regretting the Evils of This World," in *The Problem of Evil*, edited by Michael Peterson, 153–67.

Kelly, Joseph. *The Problem of Evil in the Western Tradition.* Collegeville: The Liturgical Press, 2002.

Kushner, Harold. *When Bad Things Happen to Good People.* New York: Schocken Books, 1981.

Lewis, C. S. *Perelandra.* New York: Collier Books, 1944.

Milton, John. *Paradise Lost.* New York: Maxwell Macmillan International, 1981.

Minow, Martha. *Between Vengeance and Forgiveness.* Boston: Beacon Press, 1998.

O'Connor, Flannery. *The Complete Stories.* New York: Farrar, Straus, Geroux, 1971.

Peterson, Michael, editor. *The Problem of Evil.* Notre Dame, Ind.: University of Notre Dame Press, 1992.

Pinn, Anthony, editor. *Moral Evil and Redemptive Suffering: A History of Theodicy in African-American Religious Thought.* Gainesville: University Press of Florida, 2002.

Rahner, Karl. "Why Does God Allow Us to Suffer?" in *Theological Investigations* 19, Baltimore: Helicon Press, 1983, 194–208.

Russell, Jeffrey Burton. *The Devil: Perceptions of Evil from Antiquity to Primitive Christianity.* Ithaca, N.Y.: Cornell University Press, 1977.

Shakur, Sanyika. *Monster: The Autobiography of an L.A. Gang Member.* New York: Penguin Books, 1993.

Shelley, Mary. *Frankenstein.* New York: Dover Books, 1994.

Thiel, John. *God, Evil, and Innocent Suffering: A Theological Reflection.* New York: Crossroad, 2002.

Walsch, Neale Donald. *Conversations with God: An Uncommon Dialogue, Volume One.* New York: G. W. Putnam's Sons.

Zehr, Howard. "Restoring Justice," in *God and the Victim*, edited by Lisa Barnes and Michael Shattuck, Grand Rapids, Mich.: William B. Eerdmans, 2000, 131–59.